QUICKEN
in easy s

Stephen Copestake

COMPUTER STEP

In easy steps is an imprint of Computer Step
Southfield Road . Southam
Warwickshire CV33 OFB . England

Tel: 01926 817999 Fax: 01926 817005
http://www.computerstep.com

3rd edition 1998

Notice of Liability

Every effort has been made to ensure that this book contains accurate and current information. However, Computer Step and the author shall not be liable for any loss or damage suffered by readers as a result of any information contained herein.

Trademarks

Printed and bound in the United Kingdom

ISBN 1-84078-007-X

Contents

3   Accounts   59

4   Memorising Transactions   85

First Steps

Use this chapter to learn how to have Quicken automate the setting up of your first account. Then discover how to activate commonly used features with a single mouse click, and have Quicken prompt you when bills need to be paid (or other preset criteria are met). You'll also learn how to use the HELP system, and run Overviews within Quicken itself. Finally, you'll store personal data within the Emergency Record Organiser, and discover how to work with the 'files' which underlie Quicken accounts.

Covers

Starting Quicken the first time

REMEMBER

Use standard Windows procedures to launch Quicken.

When you run Quicken for the first time, you're guided through the process of setting up a new account, easily and painlessly. The Quicken New User Setup dialog launches. Do the following:

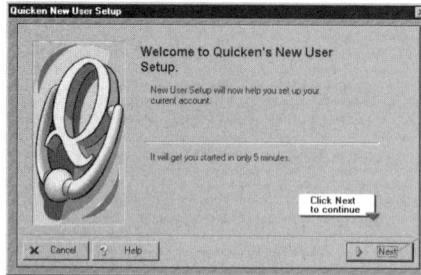

1 Click here

2 Answer these questions

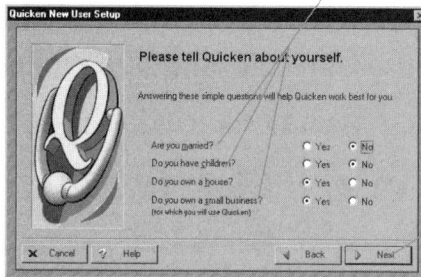

REMEMBER

Accounts are crucial in Quicken; they represent the bank or building society accounts in which you organise your finances.

3 Click here

4 Name the new account

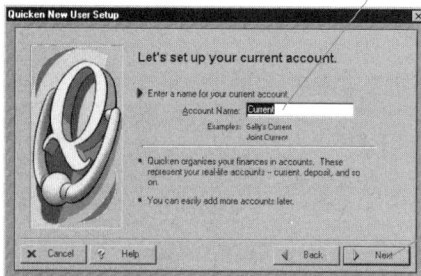

5 Click here

...cont'd

The next stage is to:

VAT tracking is beyond the scope of this book.

- tell Quicken whether VAT tracking should be in force

- choose a currency

6 Click here

Quicken assumes you want to create a bank (current) account, since these are by far the most common. There are other types. Expertise you build up with bank accounts is to a large extent transferrable, since the account types work on very similar principles.

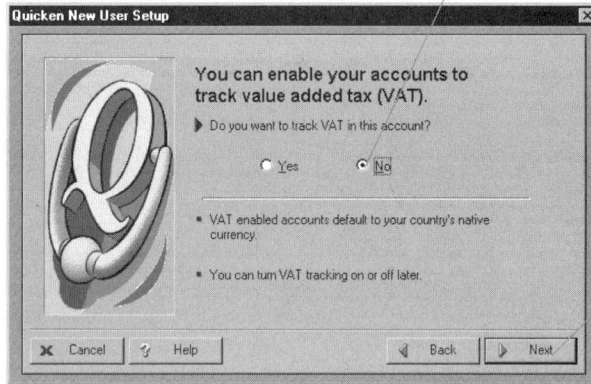

7 Click here

8 Click here; select a currency in the list

9 Click here

...cont'd

HANDY TIP

Re step 10 – if you don't have the last statement to hand:

- don't worry: the process of reconciliation (see Chapter 7) will resolve any disparity later
- note that the dialog shown below does not appear. Perform steps 10-11, but ignore 12-14. Then jump straight to page 11.

Now you:

- tell Quicken if you have your last statement to hand
- supply Quicken with the ending date and balance

Do the following:

10 Make the appropriate choice

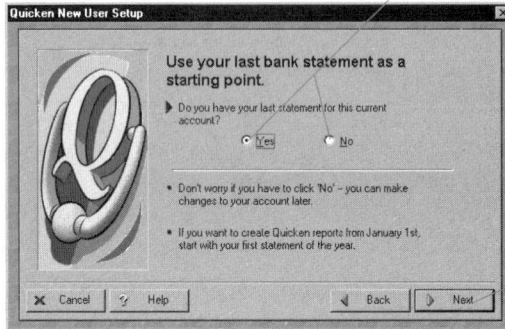

11 Click here

REMEMBER

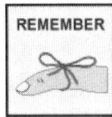

The ending date is the date of your last statement; Quicken uses this as the inception date for your new account.
The ending balance is, in the case of bank accounts, the current balance.

12 Type in the ending date

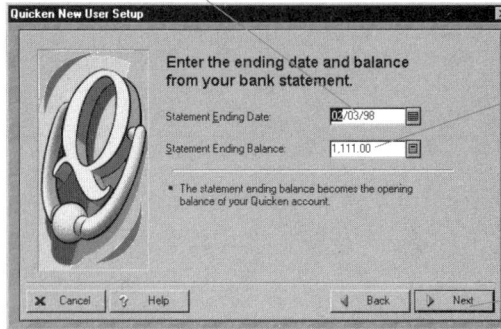

13 Type in the ending balance

14 Click here

...cont'd

In the final stage, you confirm the information you've just entered.

REMEMBER

Check the information in these fields: correct any errors. Finally, perform step 15.

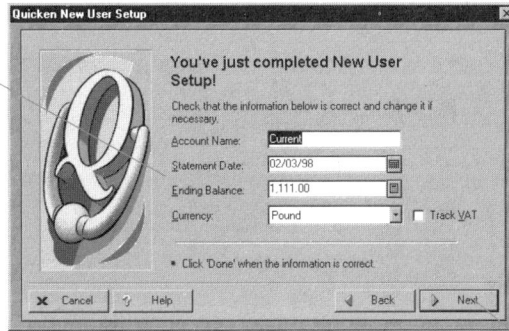

Do the following:

15 Click here

This completes the process of creating your first (and often only) account. However, you can – if you want – run a special feature known as Overviews.

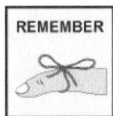

REMEMBER

See page 20 for more information on Overviews (and, in particular, on how to launch them separately).

Follow step 17 below if you *don't* want to run a Quicken Overview at this stage; this completes your first account. If, on the other hand, you do want to run one, carry out step 16, then steps 18-20 (as appropriate) on page 12:

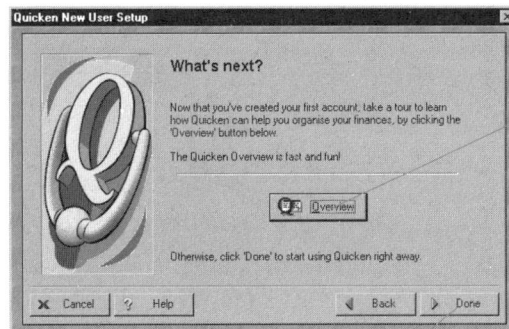

16 Click here

17 Click here

If you followed step 16 on page 11, carry out step 18 below to view a list of new features in Quicken, or steps 19-20 to run a guided tour:

18 Click here

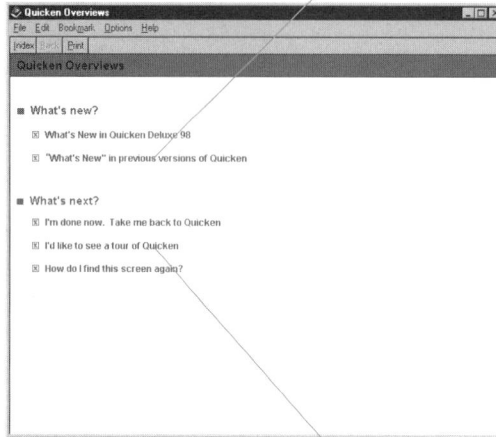

19 Click here

If you followed step 19 above, this screen launches:

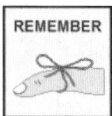

REMEMBER

Click Cancel at any time to close the Overview. Or click Done when you reach the end of the Overview to return to Quicken.

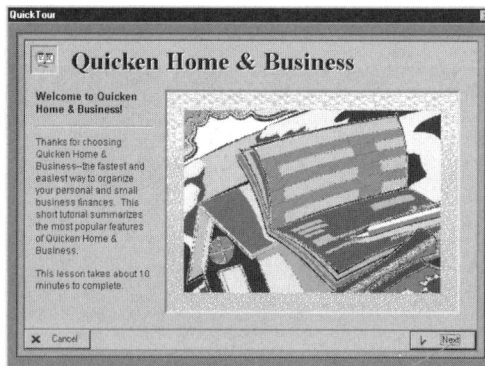

20 Click here to view the next screen

The Activity Bar and QuickTabs

Using the Activity Bar

The Activity Bar makes it even easier to access the most commonly used features and commands.

Look at the next illustration:

HANDY TIP

The icons in the Activity Bar relate to important financial tasks.
To use the Activity Bar, click an icon and make the relevant choice in the menu which launches.

QuickTabs

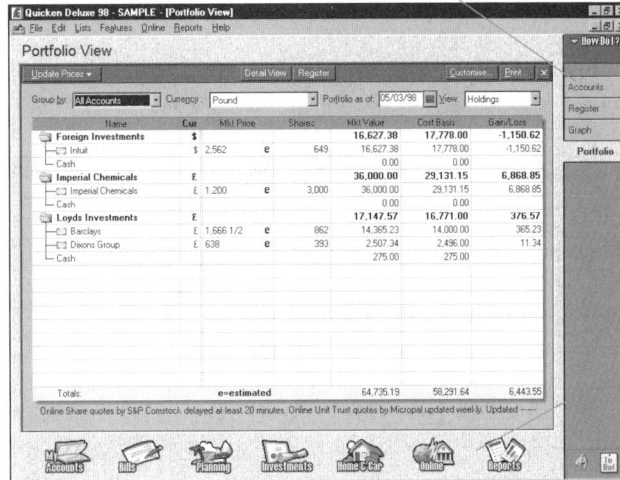

The Activity Bar – see the HANDY TIP

REMEMBER

If you're not sure which feature you want to use, click this button:

▼ How Do I?

above the QuickTabs.
In the menu which launches, click a feature (or click More for extra features, then use the resulting HELP window to locate the required information).

Using QuickTabs

QuickTabs (see the illustration above) let you jump to Quicken windows which you've already opened. Do the following:

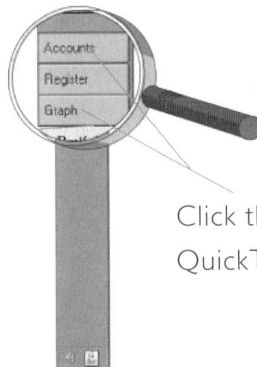

Click the appropriate QuickTab

If you want, you can force Quicken to stop displaying QuickTabs and/or the Activity Bar.

HANDY TIP

To reinstate QuickTabs or the Activity Bar, pull down the Edit menu and click Options, Quicken Program. In the General Options dialog, ensure the QuickTabs tab is active. Select Show QuickTabs and/or Show Activity Bar. Finally, click OK.

Hiding QuickTabs

Right-click over any of the visible QuickTabs. Then do the following:

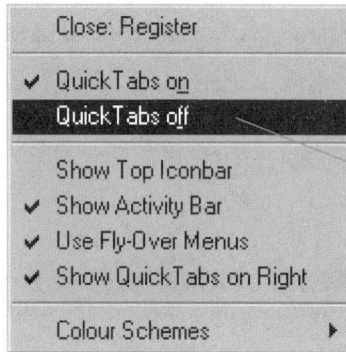

Close: Register
✔ QuickTabs on
QuickTabs off
Show Top Iconbar
✔ Show Activity Bar
✔ Use Fly-Over Menus
✔ Show QuickTabs on Right
Colour Schemes ▶

Click here

Hiding the Activity Bar

Right-click over any of the visible QuickTabs. Then do the following:

REMEMBER

**Quicken screens look quite different when QuickTabs are not displayed.
This book uses a combination of both screen types.**

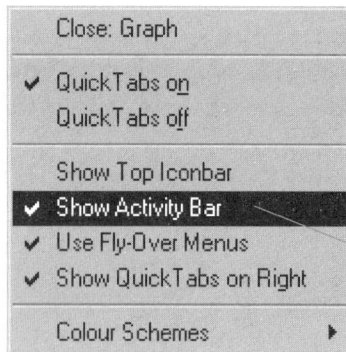

Close: Graph
✔ QuickTabs on
QuickTabs off
Show Top Iconbar
✔ Show Activity Bar
✔ Use Fly-Over Menus
✔ Show QuickTabs on Right
Colour Schemes ▶

Click here

Working with Billminder

A keynote in Quicken is automation. One of the timesaving features Quicken provides is Billminder, a cheque reminder system. Use Billminder to have Quicken remind you when cheques fall due for payment.

An important aspect of using Billminder is the number of days' notice you set. When you're considering what interval to insert, bear in mind that this should be larger than the maximum number of days between your Quicken sessions. In other words, if you only run Quicken once a week, use an interval of more than 7 days...

REMEMBER

You can write cheques manually, in the normal way, or you can have Quicken print them for you (see Chapter 6 for more information).

Setting up Billminder

Pull down the Edit menu do the following:

HANDY TIP

Re step 4 – you can turn Billminder off if you want. Simply ensure that Turn on Billminder *isn't* ticked, then follow step 5.

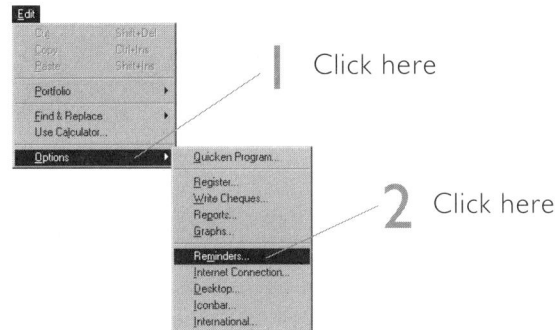

Edit menu:

| Edit |
| Shift+Del |
| Copy ... Ctrl+Ins |
| Paste ... Shift+Ins |
| Portfolio ▶ |
| Find & Replace ▶ |
| Use Calculator... |
| Options ▶ |

1 Click here

Options submenu:
- Quicken Program...
- Register...
- Write Cheques...
- Reports...
- Graphs...
- Reminders...
- Internet Connection...
- Desktop...
- Iconbar...
- International...

2 Click here

HANDY TIP

To set the Billminder reminder interval, click the Reminder tab:

In the Days in Advance: field, type in an interval. Finally, click OK.

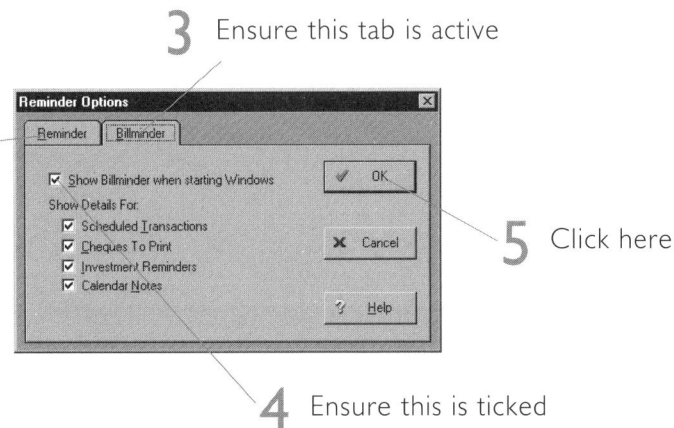

3 Ensure this tab is active

Reminder Options

Tabs: Reminder | Billminder

☑ Show Billminder when starting Windows

Show Details For:
- ☑ Scheduled Transactions
- ☑ Cheques To Print
- ☑ Investment Reminders
- ☑ Calendar Notes

Buttons: ✓ OK | ✗ Cancel | ? Help

5 Click here

4 Ensure this is ticked

Working with Alerts

You can use another Quicken feature which makes it even easier to keep on top of your finances: Alerts. Alerts are messages which automatically appear when a given situation is reached. For example, you can have Quicken inform you:

Alerts are only available if you're using the Deluxe edition of Quicken.

- when the balance in a specific account is about to reach a pre-set minimum

- when the balance actually does attain the minimum

You can also perform a similar function with regard to maximum account balances i.e. Quicken notifies you when a maximum figure you've specified has been attained. This is useful if you want to transfer account surpluses to another account which yields a higher return.

Other examples of Alerts are:

Insurance Renewal — Quicken notifies you 2 months before a premium is due, so you have plenty of time to find an alternative quote and/or review your sums insured

Mortgage Rate — Quicken notifies you 3 months before a fixed-rate mortgage becomes variable-rate. You therefore have plenty of time to consider remortgaging

Credit Card — Quicken notifies you when you're approaching a limit on a Credit Card account, and when the limit has been passed

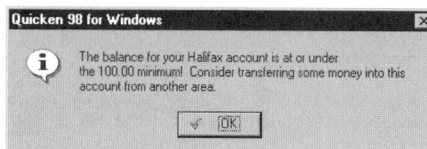

An Alert notification – note that Quicken also recommends a course of action

...cont'd

Setting up an Alert
Carry out the following steps:

HANDY TIP
Repeat steps 3-4 for as many Alerts as you want to set.

2 Click here

REMEMBER
Re. step 4 – the fields in this section of the dialog vary according to the type of Alert chosen in step 3.

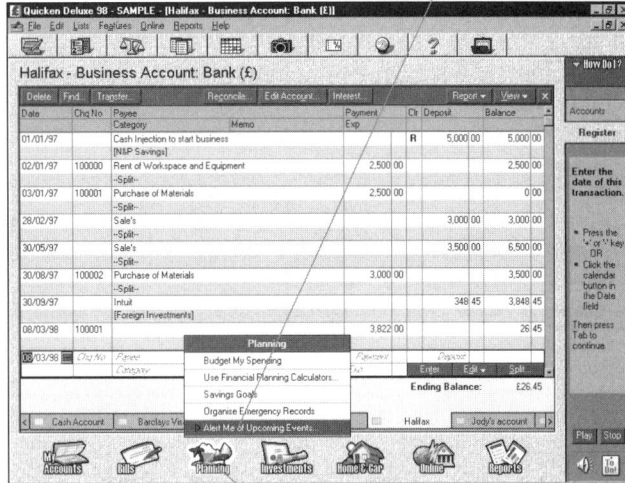

Move the mouse pointer over this icon

HANDY TIP
Re. step 3 – to activate a dormant Alert, click the box to the right. This is the result:

3 Select an Alert type

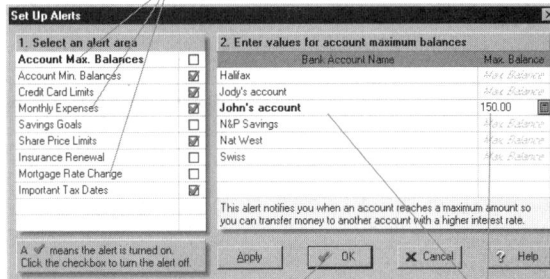

HANDY TIP
Re. step 3 – to deactivate an Alert, click the box to the right. This is the result:

5 Click here

4 Complete this section of the dialog

The Emergency Records Organiser

HANDY TIP

Consider entering data relating to topics 1-4 first, in that order.
Then complete the remaining topics in any sequence which appeals to you.

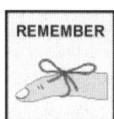

Quicken has a unique feature which you can use to keep track of vital information: the Emergency Records Organiser (ERO, for short).

The Emergency Records Organiser is a specialised, centralised, easily accessible database into which you can insert data relating to the following topics:

REMEMBER

Each topic has various sub-topics associated with it.
For instance, Adults' Emergency Information has these sub-topics:

- Contact List
- Doctors/Dentists
- Medical History
- Hospital Info

1.   Adults' emergency information

2.   Children's Emergency Information

3.   Adults' Important Information

4.   Children's Important Information

5.   Personal and Legal Documents

6.   Accounts

7.   Income

8.   Investment and Retirement

9.   Home/Motor/Property

10.   Insurance

11.   Mortgage/Loans

HANDY TIP

To print part of the ERO, click this button:

Print...

in the dialog on page 19.
Complete the Print area, topic or record dialog, as appropriate. Click Print.

You can insert information into the Emergency Records Organiser as and when you want, which makes it very convenient to use. You can also:

—   view reports relating to specific areas

—   print out your Emergency Records Organiser data, conveniently and easily

Entering data into the ERO

Open the relevant account. Pull down the Feature menu and do the following:

BEWARE **The ERO is only available if you're using the Deluxe edition of Quicken.**

HANDY TIP **To view a report, activate the Report tab. In the Report Type field, select a report; after a few seconds, Quicken displays it in the lower half of the dialog.**

HANDY TIP **To enter more data, don't follow step 7. Instead, click this button:**

New Record

Now repeat steps 4-6. Finally, perform step 7.

HANDY TIP **To close the ERO at any time, press Esc.**

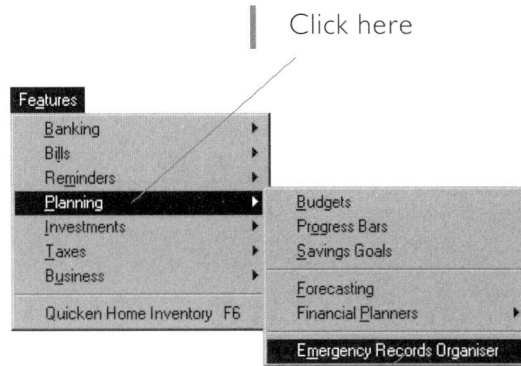

1 Click here

Features
Banking ▶
Bills ▶
Reminders ▶
Planning ▶
Investments ▶
Taxes ▶
Business ▶
Quicken Home Inventory F6

Budgets
Progress Bars
Savings Goals

Forecasting
Financial Planners ▶

Emergency Records Organiser

2 Click here

4 Click here; select a main topic in the list

3 Ensure this tab is active

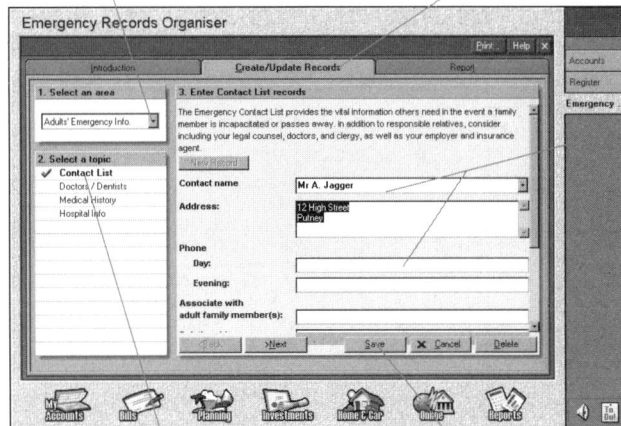

Emergency Records Organiser

| Introduction | Create/Update Records | Report |

Accounts
Register
Emergency ...

1. Select an area

Adults' Emergency Info.

2. Select a topic
✓ Contact List
   Doctors / Dentists
   Medical History
   Hospital Info

3. Enter Contact List records

The Emergency Contact List provides the vital information others need in the event a family member is incapacitated or passes away. In addition to responsible relatives, consider including your legal counsel, doctors, and clergy, as well as your employer and insurance agent.

New Record

Contact name: Mr A. Jagger

Address: 12 High Street Putney

Phone
  Day:
  Evening:

Associate with adult family member(s):

Back   >Next   Save   ✗ Cancel   Delete

6 Fill in this section

5 Click a sub-topic

7 Click here

Running Overviews separately

As we've already seen, when you run Quicken for the first time you can opt to run special in-built tutorials called Overviews. However, you can also launch Overviews independently, at any time.

Launching an Overview

Pull down the Help menu and do the following:

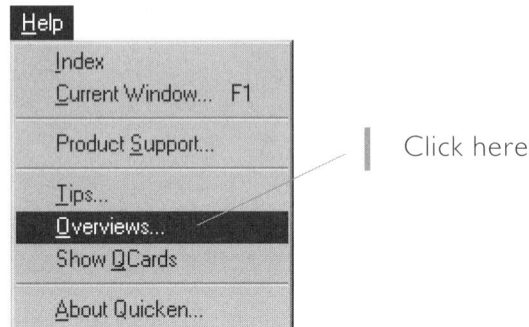

Help
Index
Current Window... F1

Product Support...

Tips...
Overviews...
Show QCards

About Quicken...

Click here

2 Click an Overview
to launch it

REMEMBER

After step 2, follow the relevant on-screen instructions.

HANDY TIP

To close any Overview (or the window on the right), press Esc.

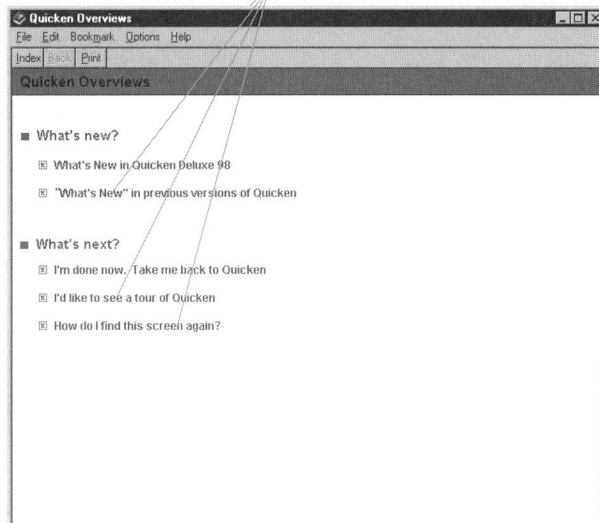

Quicken Overviews
File Edit Bookmark Options Help
Index Back Print
Quicken Overviews

■ What's new?

⊠ What's New in Quicken Deluxe 98

⊠ "What's New" in previous versions of Quicken

■ What's next?

⊠ I'm done now. Take me back to Quicken

⊠ I'd like to see a tour of Quicken

⊠ How do I find this screen again?

Using HELP Contents

Quicken has comprehensive Help facilities, organised under two broad headings:

* Contents (a list of topics organised thematically)

* Index (an alphabetical list of topics)

To generate the Help Contents dialog, pull down the Help menu and choose Index.

Using Contents

Do the following:

You can use a keyboard shortcut to launch Help: simply press F1.
Click the Index or Contents tabs, as appropriate, and then follow the relevant steps.

Click this tab

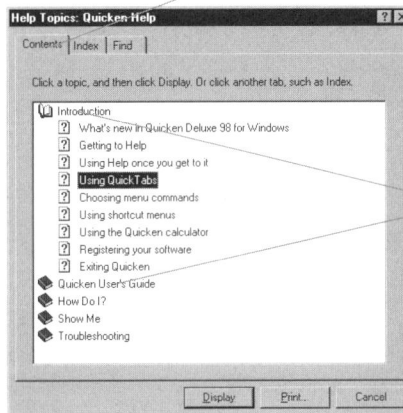

Help Topics: Quicken Help

Contents | Index | Find

Click a topic, and then click Display. Or click another tab, such as Index.

Introduction
    What's new in Quicken Deluxe 98 for Windows
    Getting to Help
    Using Help once you get to it
    Using QuickTabs
    Choosing menu commands
    Using shortcut menus
    Using the Quicken calculator
    Registering your software
    Exiting Quicken
Quicken User's Guide
How Do I?
Show Me
Troubleshooting

Display   Print...   Cancel

2 Double-click the relevant heading

After step 2, Quicken launches a series of sub-headings. When you find the topic you want information on (prefixed by ⟨?⟩ instead of ⟨📖⟩), double-click it. Quicken launches the appropriate HELP window.

Sometimes step 2 produces a different (expanded) HELP window.
Simply follow the on-screen instructions.

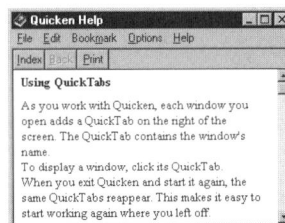

Quicken Help

File Edit Bookmark Options Help

Index | Back | Print

Using QuickTabs

As you work with Quicken, each window you open adds a QuickTab on the right of the screen. The QuickTab contains the window's name.
To display a window, click its QuickTab.
When you exit Quicken and start it again, the same QuickTabs reappear. This makes it easy to start working again where you left off.

A sample HELP window – press Esc when you've finished using it

Using HELP Index

To generate the Help Index dialog, pull down the Help menu and choose Index.

Using Index
Do the following:

HANDY TIP

You can use a keyboard shortcut to launch Help: simply press F1.
Click the Index or Contents tabs, as appropriate, and then follow the relevant steps.

| Type in a key word or phrase

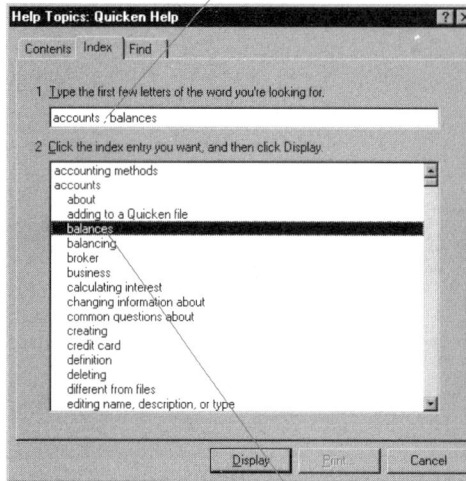

2 Double-click the relevant topic

REMEMBER

Sometimes, carrying out step 2 produces a list of topics:

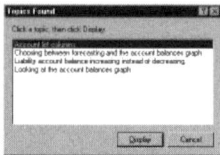

After step 2, Quicken launches a HELP window (but see the REMEMBER tip on the left):

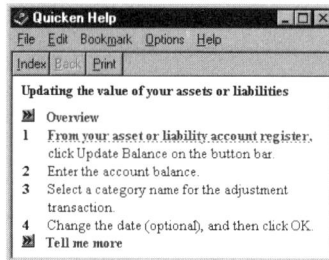

Simply double-click a topic to launch the appropriate HELP window.

A sample HELP window – press Esc when you've finished using it

Quicken Tips

Quicken has an additional feature which makes it even easier to find relevant assistance: Quicken Tips. This is a special dialog which provides a list of hints and tips. You can:

- cycle through available tips, one at a time

- view a complete list

- view the complete HELP topic which relates to a specific tip

- have the Quicken Tips dialog display automatically each time you run Quicken

Using Quicken Tips

Pull down the Help menu and click Quicken Tips. Now carry out any of steps 1-3 below. Finally, follow step 4.

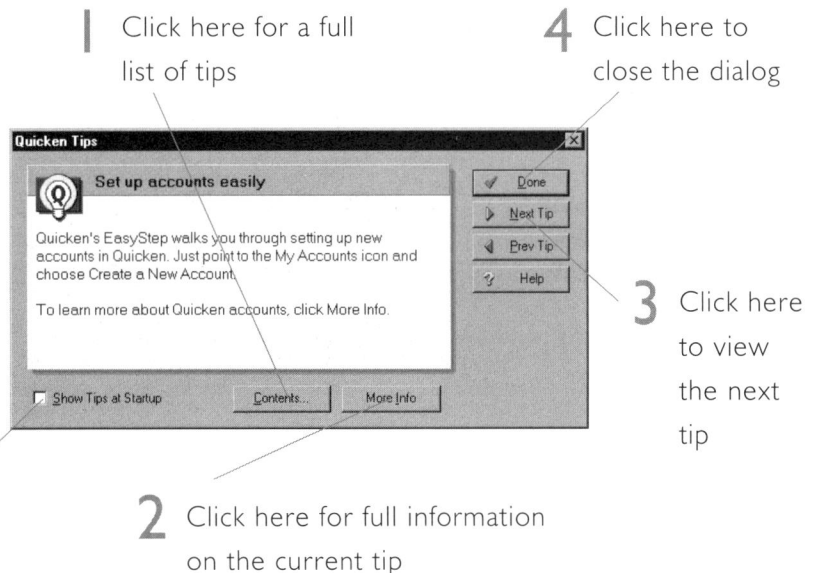

1 Click here for a full list of tips

4 Click here to close the dialog

3 Click here to view the next tip

Click here: to have the Quicken Tips dialog launch whenever you run Quicken.

2 Click here for full information on the current tip

Flyover tips

Another very useful feature in Quicken is the use of 'flyover' help. Flyover help displays explanatory text when you move the mouse pointer over icons in the on-screen Iconbar:

Create a report of your finances

Ensuring that flyover help is active

If the above procedure doesn't work, pull down the Edit menu and click Options, Quicken Program.

Do the following:

HANDY TIP

If the Iconbar isn't currently on screen, pull down the Edit menu and click Options, Iconbar. In the Customize Iconbar dialog, click Show Icons and/or Show Text.

Finally, click OK.

2 Click here

General Options

QuickTabs | General | Settings

QuickTabs
☑ Show QuickTabs

Position
○ On the Left   ● On the Right
☑ Show Activity Bar
☐ Use Short Commands on Activity Bar Menus

Quicken Colour   Default 256-colour
☑ Show Flyover Help in Toolbars

✓ OK
✗ Cancel
? Help

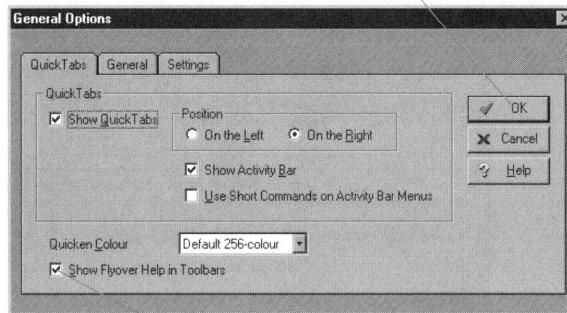

Ensure this is selected

The Quicken Iconbar:

Qcards

HANDY TIP

Qcards are very useful when you're new to Quicken. When you're more experienced, however, you may find they're a distraction. In this case, simply repeat step 1 on the right to disable Qcards.

Qcards are a specialised HELP feature which resembles flyover tips. When you move the insertion point into the majority of fields in Quicken accounts, an explanatory box pops up with context-specific help.

Turning on the Qcards feature

Pull down the Help menu and do the following:

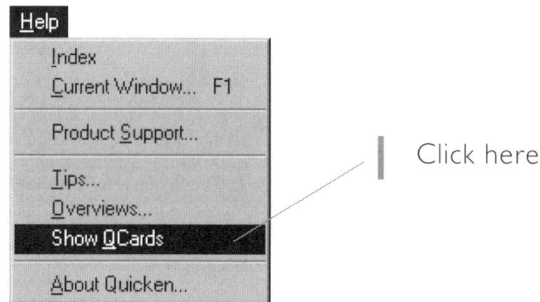

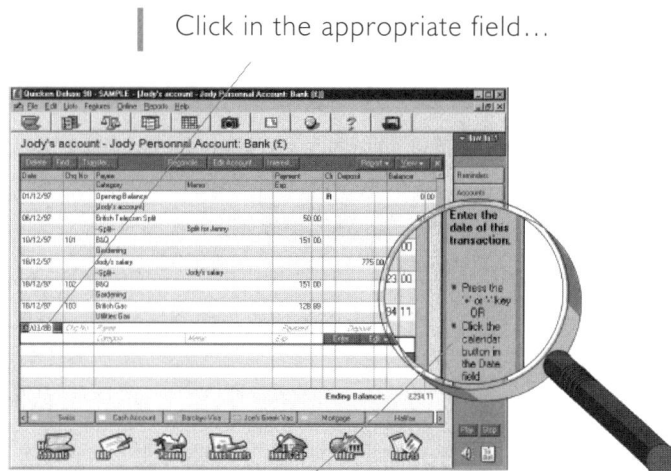

Help
Index
Current Window... F1
Product Support...
Tips...
Overviews...
Show QCards
About Quicken...

Click here

Using Qcards

Do the following:

Click in the appropriate field...

Quicken displays the relevant Qcard

Files – an overview

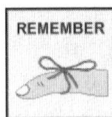

Here is some more basic Quicken terminology (these terms are discussed in greater detail later).

Accounts **are collections of transactions (withdrawals or deposits).**

The Register **is the window through which transactions are entered into an account, and strongly resembles a bank statement.**

Categories **and** **classes** **are useful classifying labels which can be attached to transactions.**

Each Quicken file actually consists of several files. However, you don't need to concern yourself with these: Quicken manages the various components behind the scenes.

Files are crucial to the way Quicken works. However, it places a special interpretation on the word. In Quicken, files are collections of (usually related) accounts. For example, you may have one account which relates to domestic finance, and another which relates to a small business. Since both accounts relate to *you* (and additionally may well have a crossover in terms of money transferred between them), Quicken organises them under the aegis of a single file.

Quicken creates a file automatically (known as QDATA) when you create your first account (see the 'Starting Quicken the first time' topics earlier). Many users never need to create another; however, you can do so if you want to – for instance, if you run more than one business it may well be useful to have separate files for each.

You can also:

• backup and restore files

• copy files

• rename files

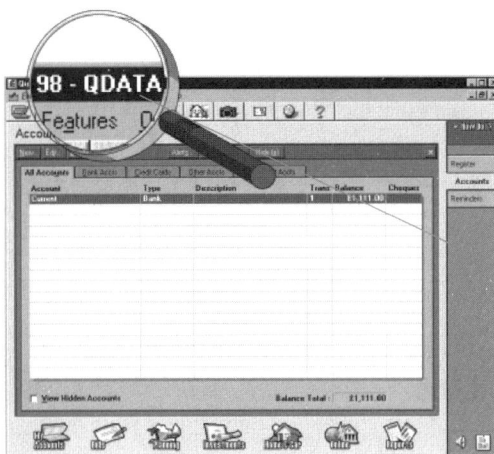

Magnified view of menu bar entry giving details of the underlying file

Creating new files

To create a new file, pull down the File menu and click New. Now do the following:

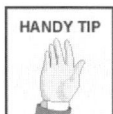

Click here

Creating new file: Are you sure?

Create

- New Quicken File
  A Quicken file is a collection of accounts, categories, memorised items, and so on.

- New Quicken Account
  A Quicken account is a list of transactions for a single current account, credit card or other financial item.

✔ OK

✘ Cancel

? Help

HANDY TIP

Before you carry out step 4, click this button:

Categories...

In the Quicken Categories dialog, select one or more category groups which you wish associated with your new file. Click OK.

(For how to use categories, see Chapter 2).

2 Click here

4 Click here

Create Quicken File

Save in: quickenw

- Backup
- Dat
- inet
- plugins
- sample
- sounds
- Qdata.qdf

File name: New

Save as type: Quicken Files (*.QDF)

Categories...

OK

Cancel

Help

HANDY TIP

After step 4, Quicken assumes that you want to create the first account for your new file.

If you want to do this, refer to Chapter 3.

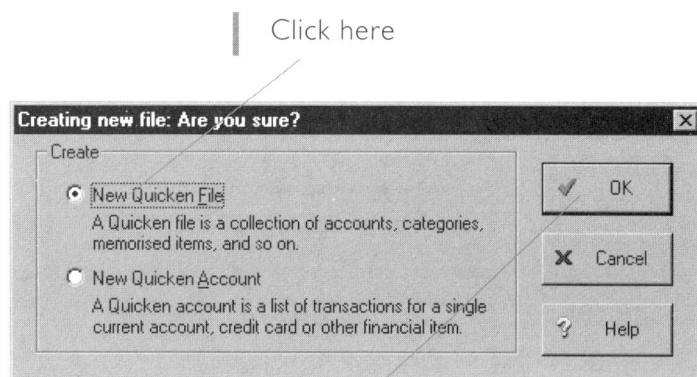

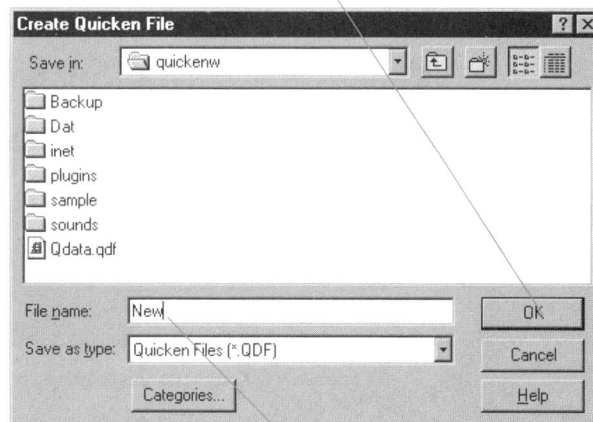

3 Name the new file

Opening files

If you've created more than one Quicken file (maybe because you run more than one business, or because you wanted to emphasise differing accounting periods), you'll need to open the specific file you need to work with.

HANDY TIP

If you only use the default file QDATA, you don't need to open it: Quicken does this for you when you run the program.

Do the following:

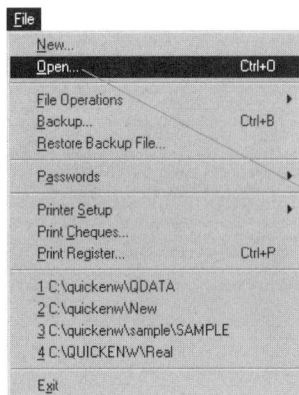

File	
New...	
Open...	Ctrl+O
File Operations	▶
Backup...	Ctrl+B
Restore Backup File...	
Passwords	▶
Printer Setup	▶
Print Cheques...	
Print Register...	Ctrl+P
1 C:\quickenw\QDATA	
2 C:\quickenw\New	
3 C:\quickenw\sample\SAMPLE	
4 C:\QUICKENW\Real	
Exit	

Click here

3 Click here

Open Quicken File   ? X

Look in: 📁 quickenw

- 📁 Backup   📄 New.QDF
- 📁 Dat   📄 Qdata.qdf
- 📁 inet
- 📁 plugins
- 📁 sample
- 📁 sounds
- 📄 ~qw~link.qdt

File name: New.QDF   OK

Files of type: Quicken Files (*.QDF;*.QDB;*.QDT)   Cancel

                                          Help

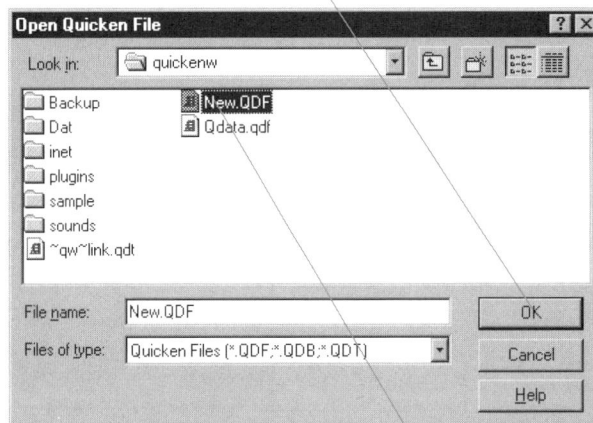

2 Highlight a file

Backing up files

HANDY TIP

It's good policy to maintain *two* independent backup copies of your data.

As you work with your Quicken file(s), it's important to *back up* your work regularly. Backing up is the process of copying data stored on your hard disk to a floppy disk so that, if any hardware- or software-based errors result in data loss, you can get back to the situation you were in before the loss. Quicken makes carrying out backups easy and convenient.

First, open the file you want to back up and place a floppy disk in the relevant drive. Pull down the File menu and carry out the following steps:

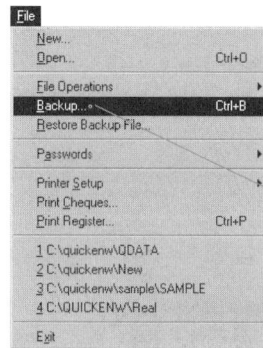

HANDY TIP

After step 1, Quicken launches this message:

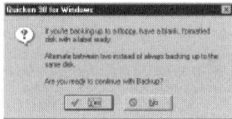

Click Yes, then follows steps 2-4.

Click here

BEWARE

If you're backing up onto a disk already used for this purpose, Quicken launches a warning:

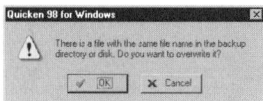

if the file name is the same.
Click OK to overwrite the original backup file.

4 Click here

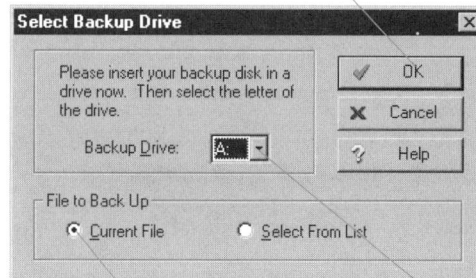

2 Ensure this is selected

3 Click here; select a target drive from the list

Restoring files

Restoring files is the process of reinstating backed up data (in the case of loss or damage to the original) onto your hard disk. Hopefully, you'll never have to do this. If you do, however, you can take comfort from the fact that Quicken makes the process very easy.

First, place the latest backup floppy disk in the relevant drive. Pull down the File menu and carry out the following steps:

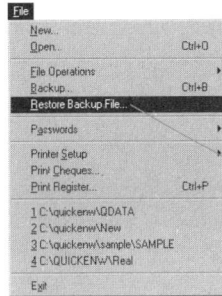

Click here

 **Restore can also be used to copy data onto a _different_ hard disk. This equates to a way of transferring data between separate computers. However, both computers must have Quicken installed on them.**

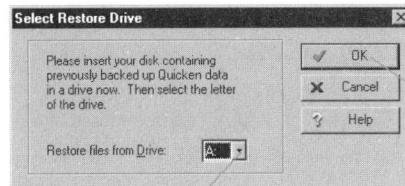

3 Click here

2 Click the arrow; select the backup drive in the list

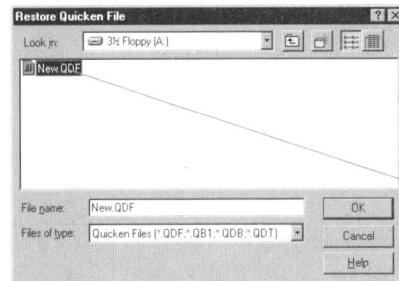

4 Double-click the file you want to restore

Additional file operations

It's sometimes important to undertake file housekeeping. This can involve any of the following:

File copying

Pull down the File menu and click File Operations, Copy. Now do the following:

HANDY TIP

When you copy a file, you can determine which transactions are included by specifying a date range – see step 2.

Name the new copy

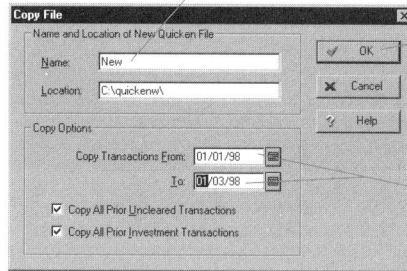

3 Click here

2 Optional – enter transaction dates

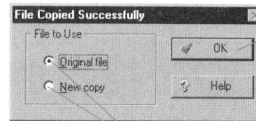

REMEMBER

Copying a file has another benefit: it prunes it by deleting unused records. As a result, the file size is reduced.

5 Click here

4 Select which file you want Quicken to open

File renaming

Pull down the File menu and click File Operations, Rename. Now do the following:

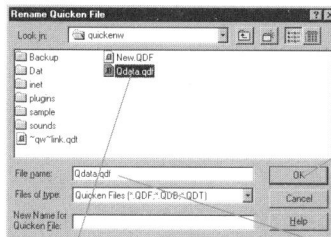

3 Click here

2 Type in the new name

Click the file you want to rename

File deleting

If necessary, you can delete a Quicken file (but see the BEWARE tip).

Pull down the File menu and click File Operations, Delete. Now do the following:

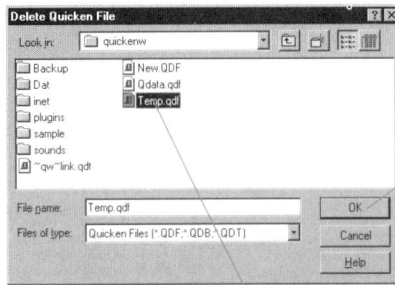

BEWARE

Once a file has been deleted, it's gone for good.

However, you can restore the latest of a series of backup copies which Quicken automatically creates (every 7 days) in your QUICKENW\BACKUP\ **folder.**

Even better, if you create backups on floppy disks every time you close a Quicken session, you can restore the latest of these, which will minimise data loss even more.

(See p. 30 for how to restore files.)

2 Click here

Click the file you want to delete

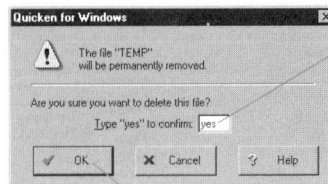

3 Type in 'yes' (omit the quote marks)

4 Click here

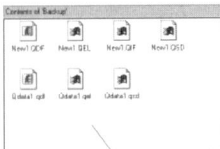

A Backup folder, viewed in Windows Explorer

File validating

If you experience any problems with a file, you *may* be able to have Quicken correct them.

Pull down the File menu and click File Operations, Validate. Use the Validate Quicken File dialog to locate the suspect fie; click OK. Now follow the on-screen instructions.

The Register

Use this chapter to acquire the basics of entering transactions into the Register. You'll monitor your finances dynamically, and classify transactions (for greater precision) by applying categories/sub-categories, and classes/sub-classes; you'll also create your own. You'll learn how to undertake category and class housekeeping. Finally, you'll 'split' complex transactions into their constituent components, to ensure that your accounts represent the totality of your finances.

Chapter Two

Covers

Transactions – an overview

The following points are central to the way Quicken works:

- Quicken defines a transaction as anything which affects the balance of an account

- you enter transactions into the Register, a special window which resembles a chequebook and lets you access the account

- within the account, transactions are entered into *fields*. The main fields are:

    - Date

    - Chq No

    - Payee

    - Payment

    - Deposit

    - Category (used to classify transactions)

    - Memo (used to add explanatory text for descriptive purposes)

Payee	
Category	Memo
Opening Balance	
[Current]	

Excerpted fields

Some of the principal transaction types are:

— cheques/deposits

— bank charges

— accrued interest

— cash dispenser withdrawals

Entering transactions

Entering data into accounts is easy. Carry out the following steps:

Click in a field and type in the relevant data

REMEMBER **Repeat step 1 for each necessary field within the relevant transaction.**

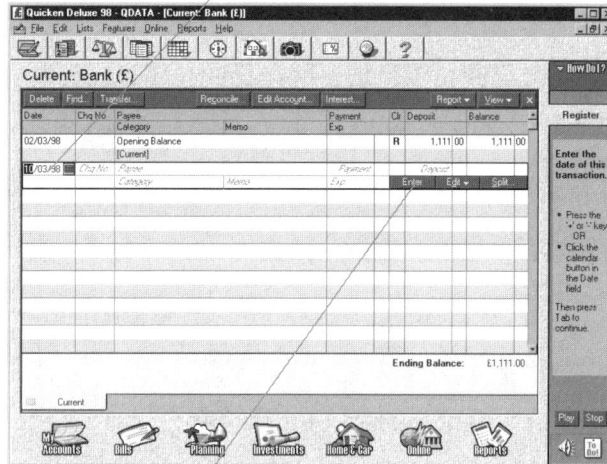

2 Click here to record your transaction

HANDY TIP **Two other useful shortcuts are:**

***Ctrl+Home* – moves to the first transaction in the account.**
***Ctrl+End* – moves to the very last transaction.**

Moving to fields

To enter data into a field, you can simply click in it and begin typing. If a field isn't visible, use the scroll bars to rectify this. However, you can also use keyboard routes to find the appropriate field. The simplest method is to use the cursor keys to move through accounts, but there are also shortcuts:

Tab	moves the insertion point to the next field
Shift+Tab	reverses the direction of movement
Ctrl+Page Up	moves to the first transaction in the current month
Ctrl+Page Down	moves to the last transaction in the current month

You can also use a shortcut to enter transactions: QuickFill.

Using QuickFill

QuickFill is a useful feature which speeds up the entering of data. When you click in some fields, a boxed arrow appears. Do the following:

REMEMBER

See Chapter 4 for more information on how to use QuickFill .

Click the arrow; in the list,
select a preset option

Sometimes, the list is graphical:

Here, clicking the little graphic – ▦ – has produced
a calendar; to insert a date, simply click it

HANDY TIP

Click these arrows to move to the previous or next month.

Advanced Register sorting

Normally, you enter transactions into the Register in date order. This is the most convenient – and logical – method. However, Quicken lets you view entered data in a variety of additional ways. You can have transactions sorted:

- by amount (in descending order)

- by amount (in ascending order)

- by cheque number

- alphabetically, by payee

- by date-entry order (i.e. the date you entered transactions, NOT their effective date)

- by effective date, and then by date entered (i.e. transactions are viewed in effective date order; those with the same effective date, however, are sorted in date-entry order)

- by effective date, and then by amount (i.e. transactions are viewed in effective date order; those with the same effective date, however, are sorted in amount order)

- by cleared status (reconciled transactions take priority)

REMEMBER **See chapter 7 for how to reconcile accounts.**

Sorting the Register

Within the Register, do the following:

Click here

Now carry out the following additional step:

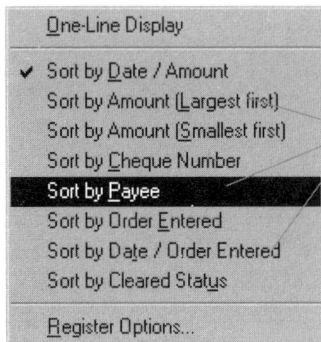

| One-Line Display |
| Sort by Date / Amount ✔ |
| Sort by Amount (Largest first) |
| Sort by Amount (Smallest first) |
| Sort by Cheque Number |
| Sort by Payee |
| Sort by Order Entered |
| Sort by Date / Order Entered |
| Sort by Cleared Status |
| Register Options... |

2 Click a sort type

Example:

In the following illustration, transactions are being sorted in date-entry order:

Date	Chq No	Payee		Payment	Clr	Deposit	Balance	
		Category	Memo	Exp				
10/12/97	101	B&Q		151 00			-151 00	
		Gardening						
18/12/97	102	B&Q		151 00			-302 00	
		Gardening						
18/12/97	103	British Gas		128 89			-430 89	
		Utilities:Gas						
06/12/97		British Telecom Split		50 00			-480 89	
		--Split--	Split for Jenny					
18/12/97		Jody's salary				775 00	294 11	
		--Split--	Jody's salary					
16/03/98	Chq No	Payee		Payment		Deposit		
		Category	Memo	Exp				

Ending Balance: £294.11

Here, date-entry order produces results which are slightly different from effective-date order...

Single-line view

Normally, Quicken's Register displays transactions on two lines. This is often convenient. However, there are situations when it may be more productive to view them on a single line.

REMEMBER

When you implement single-line view, its effect is restricted to the currently open account.

For example, if a Quicken account becomes unusually complex, you may find it easier to work with each transaction on one line. When you do this, Quicken:

1. moves the Category field onto the same line as the Payee field

2. hides the Memo field

Transactions displayed
on a single line

HANDY TIP

To return to two-line display, repeat the procedures outlined here.

Changing to single-line view

Within the Register, click this button in the overhead Button bar:

In the menu which appears, click One-Line Display.

The Net Worth pop-up

You can use a unique aid to keep abreast of your current net worth: the Net Worth pop-up. This is a specialised bar which sits on top of your Quicken screen (it even displays above other program windows, too) and supplies a dynamically up-to-date summary of your overall finances.

HANDY TIP

To specify the accounts and date ranges on which the Net Worth pop-up bases its summary, click this button:
  Complete the Customize Balance Box dialog, as appropriate. Finally, click OK.

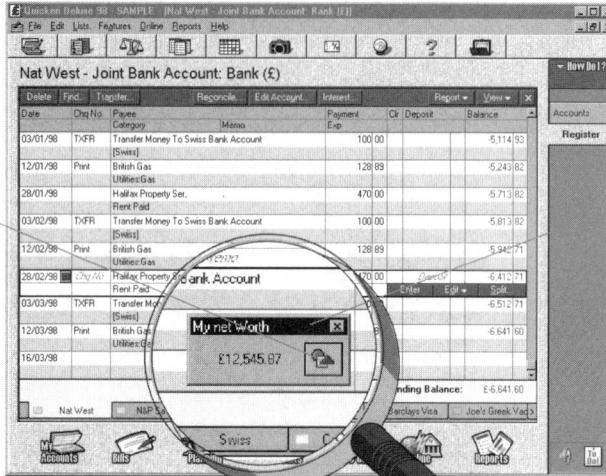

Net Worth pop-up

Launching the Net Worth pop-up

HANDY TIP

Repeat steps 1-2 to hide the Net Worth pop-up.

If the Net Worth pop-up isn't currently visible, pull down the Features menu and do the following:

Click here

2 Click here

Categories – an overview

Traditional book-based accounts make use of identifying headings – for instance, outgoings are entered as 'Stationery' or 'Drawings'. Quicken takes this practice and extends it almost infinitely, and with much more detail. It does this by allowing you to assign 'categories' to transactions.

REMEMBER

Categories fall into two broad divisions:
• Income (applied to deposits)
• Expense (applied to withdrawals)

Categories are convenient labels; you can – and should – use them to:

- organise your accounts and make them much more detailed

- produce tailor-made reports – see Chapter 8 for more information

- produce customised graphs – see Chapter 8 for more information

Limiting reports or graphs to specific categories produces a much more precise result.

Sub-categories

To ensure even greater precision, categories can – and very often are – divided into sub-categories. For example, the Income category Old Age Pension is split into:

— Employer

— State

for obvious reasons.

HANDY TIP

Quicken comes with a large number of categories and sub-categories. However, you can easily create your own.

See the 'Creating categories' topics later.

Terminology

Quicken differentiates between categories and sub-categories by separating them with a colon. Look at the following:

Utilities:Water

The entry to the left of the colon is the category, that to the right the sub-category.

Using categories/sub-categories

The use of categories and sub-categories makes for great precision. However, you need to exercise some care in how you apply them.

For example, if you're entering a payment to your regional water company into your account, you'll probably apply the following preset combination:

Utilities:Water

By doing this, you ensure that there is no possible doubt as to the identity of the withdrawal. However, when you come to have Quicken compile a report, you may well not need this level of precision. It will probably be sufficient merely to have the report based on *all* Utilities payments...

Applying categories and sub-categories

Within the relevant transaction in an account, do the following:

Click here

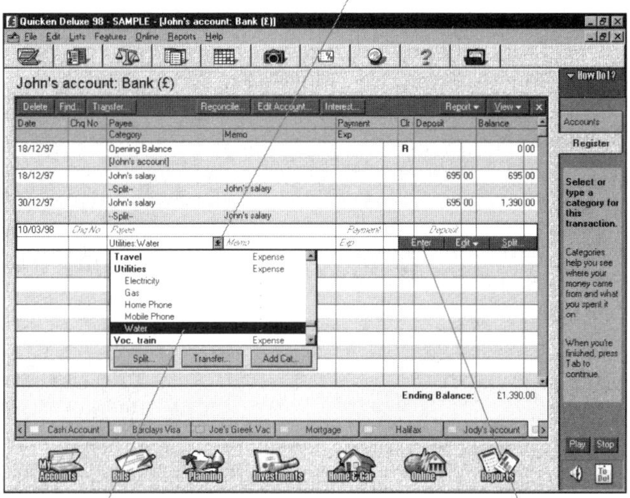

2 Select a category or category/sub-category

3 Click here to record the transaction

Creating categories/sub-categories

HANDY TIP

Category/ sub- category names can now have as many as 32 characters.

For instance, you could create a new category/sub-category combination with the following name:
Rent:Relating to 84 High St, Peckham

If, on the other hand, you tried to created the following:
Rent:Relating to 84 High Sreet, Peckham
Quicken would refuse to accept it because the 32-character limit has been exceeded.

When you allocate categories and/or sub-categories to your transactions, you can select from a large number of ready-made choices which cover most conceivable situations, in both domestic and commercial use. In the early stages of your use of Quicken, this will certainly be sufficient. As your experience increases, however, you'll probably want to create your own.

Creating categories and sub-categories is easy and convenient, and even fun. There are two methods, the formal and the informal (a shortcut).

The formal method

Quicken provides a special dialog which you can use to create categories for future use.

Pull down the Lists menu and click Category & Transfer. Do the following:

Click here

Category & Transfer List					
New... Edit... Delete			Super... Add... [+]		Report Close
All Categories	Income Categories	Expence Categories	Account Transfers		
Category	**Type**	**Tax**	**Description**		**VAT**
Bonus	**Inc**	**Tax**	**Bonus Income**		
Business income	Inc	Tax	Gross income / turnover		S
Dist. rec'd	Sub	Tax	Distribution received		
Other trusts	Sub	Tax	Discretionary, Estate...		
Sales	Sub				S
CapGnDst	Inc	Tax	Cap Gain Dist		
Capital gains	Inc	Tax	Amount received		
Child Benefit	Inc	Tax	Child Benefit		
Div Income	Inc	Tax	Dividend Income		
Ord dividend	Sub	Tax	Ordinary dividends		
Stock dividend	Sub	Tax	Stock dividends		
Employment	Inc	Tax	Employment income		
Benefits	Sub	Tax	Benefits		
Foreign	Sub	Tax	Foreign salary & wages		
Lump sums	Sub	Tax	Lump sum payments		
Other employ.	Sub	Tax	Tips, casual pmts, other.		
Salary & wages	Sub	Tax	Salary & wages		
Foreign	Inc	Tax	Foreign Income		

REMEMBER

This is how the Category & Transfer List looks if Quicken's QuickTabs feature isn't activated.

(For how to turn QuickTabs on and off, see pages 13-14).

Now carry out the additional steps overleaf.

The formal method requires completion of a further dialog.

Carry out step 2, then do one of the following:

- if you're creating a category, follow step 3 (to specify the category type).

- if, on the other hand, you're creating a sub-category, follow steps 4 and 5 (this selects the category to which the new sub-category is attached) instead

Finally – in either case – carry out step 6:

HANDY TIP **Optional – you can type in descriptive text here, for identification purposes:**

2 Name the new category or sub-category

3 Click Income or Expense

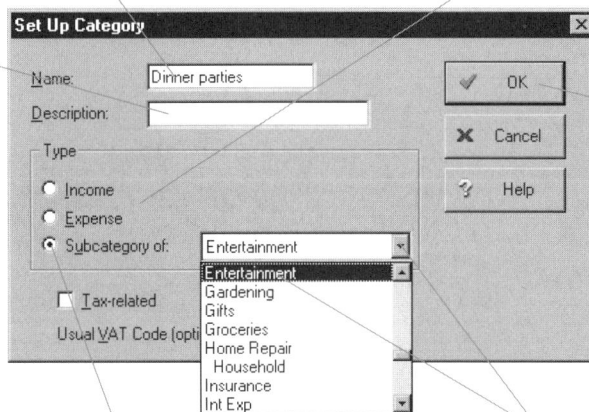

Set Up Category

Name: Dinner parties

Description:

Type
- Income
- Expense
- Subcategory of: Entertainment

Entertainment
Gardening
Gifts
Groceries
Home Repair
  Household
Insurance
Int Exp

Tax-related

Usual VAT Code (opti

✓ OK
✗ Cancel
❓ Help

6 Click here

4 If you're creating a sub-category, click here

5 If you're creating a sub-category, click the arrow; select the host category in the list

The informal method

You don't need to use the Category & Transfer List dialog to create a new category or sub-category. Instead, you can do it on-the-fly, directly from within the active account.

Using this shortcut method saves time and effort; it's something you'll want to do as your proficiency with Quicken increases...

Within the current account, do the following:

BEWARE

Don't forget to click this button:

`Enter`

when you've finished entering your transaction.

| Click in the Category field in the transaction you're working with

REMEMBER

After step 2, Quicken launches a special message. Do the following:

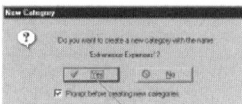

Click here

Quicken now launches the Set Up Category dialog. Follow steps 2-6 (as appropriate) on page 44.

2 Type in a name for the new category, then press Return once or twice, as necessary

Using additional categories

When you ran Quicken for the first time, you created a default account: QDATA. In the process, Quicken automatically allocated a personalised range of categories, based on your answers to the various questions it put to you. However, you can vary this allocation, at any time, by adding categories from several additional lists.

Pull down the Lists menu and click Category & Transfer List. Carry out steps 1-4 below (repeat steps 3 and 4 as often as necessary). Finally, follow step 5.

By default, Quicken applies categories from the Standard group.
The following additional groups are available in step 2:

- Married
- Homeowner
- Business
- Children
- Investment

| Click here

2 Click here; select a category group in the list

3 Click a category

Re step 3 – click the Mark All button if you want to include *all* categories within the selected group.

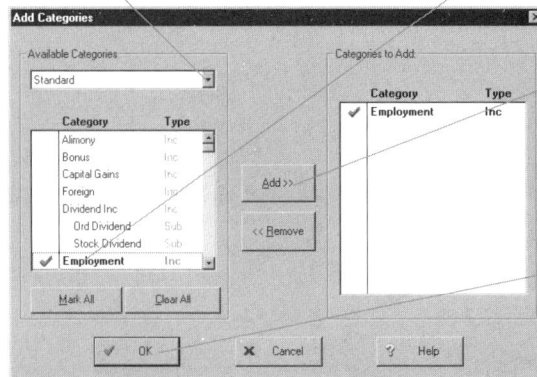

4 Click here

5 Click here

Classes – an overview

REMEMBER **Quicken comes with a large number of pre-defined categories and sub-categories, but with no classes or sub-classes (you have to set up your own).**

HANDY TIP **Quicken *does* however offer the following preset category/sub-category combination:**
Utilities:Mobile Phone
which may be suitable.

Quicken has another feature you can use to make your transactions even more precise: classes.

It's important to be clear about the distinction between classes and categories. Categories make it very easy to classify transactions, but they can sometimes be restrictive. Take the case of a small business proprietor working from home. He'll clearly have to pay both domestic and commercial telephone charges, but there will be a need to distinguish between the two. Quicken has the following preset category/sub-category:

Utilities:Home Phone

but no category/sub-category combination relating to business use. Of course, he could create a new additional category/sub-category combination e.g.:

Utilities:Work Phone

but, although this is a perfectly practicable solution, it may well be better and more convenient to create a new class instead.

Classes offer as much precision as categories: they can be further divided into sub-classes. However, they have two further advantages:

• whereas categories can be *either* Income or Expense, classes can encompass both

• classes can be used to apply broader distinctions

Like categories, classes and sub-classes can be created in two ways:

— from within a separate dialog

— on-the-fly, from within the active transaction

Creating classes

The formal method

Pull down the Lists menu and click Class. Carry out the following steps:

HANDY TIP Sub-classes appear in the Class List dialog as classes.

Click here

HANDY TIP When you've finished using the Class List dialog, press Esc to close it.

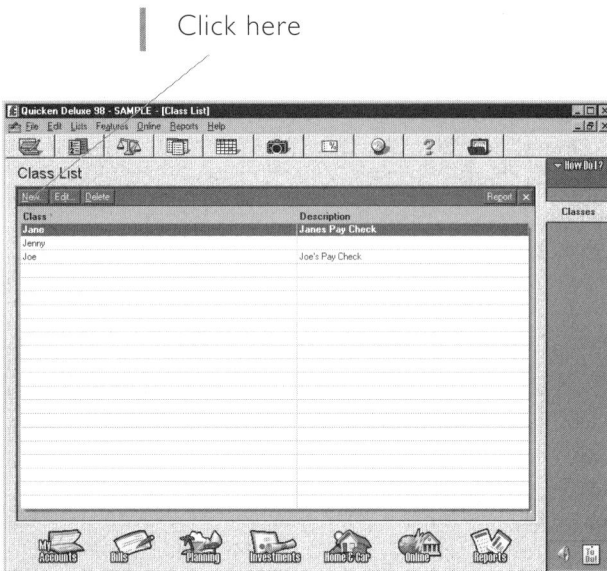

2 Name the new class

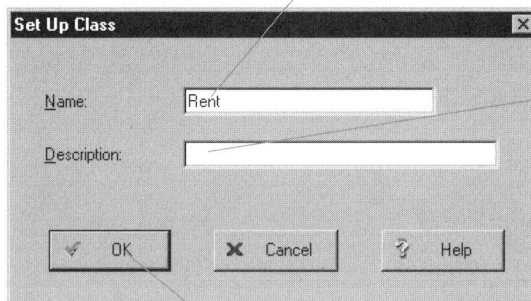

3 Optional – type in a brief description

4 Click here

The informal method

You don't need to use the Class List dialog to create a new class or sub-class. Instead, you can do it on-the-fly, directly from within the active account.

Using this shortcut method saves time and effort; it's something you'll want to do as your proficiency with Quicken increases...

Within the current account, do the following:

Don't forget to click this button:

Enter

when you've finished entering your transaction.

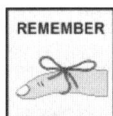

Re. step 2 – when you enter class details, prefix them with / and separate classes and sub-classes with a colon.
  For instance, to create a new class 'Home' with a sub-class 'Telephone', type in:
/Home:Telephone

Click in the Category field in the transaction you're working with

2 Type in a name for the new class, prefixed by / (see the REMEMBER tip)

If you're creating a sub-class as well as a class, Quicken launches two instances of the Set Up Class dialog; complete both in line with steps 2-4 on page 48.

Press Return once or twice, as necessary. Quicken launches the Set Up Class dialog. Follow steps 2-4 (as appropriate) on page 48.

Using classes

Using classes and sub-classes to classify your transactions is easy. However, you should bear the following in mind:

- in the early days of your use of Quicken, you probably won't need to use classes and sub-classes. However, they will be invaluable later

- classes/sub-classes *complement* (but don't replace) the use of categories/sub-categories

REMEMBER

Quicken doesn't ship with preset classes or sub-classes – you have to create your own before you can use them.
(See the pages 48-49 for how to do this.)

Applying a class

Within the appropriate account, do the following:

1 Click in the relevant Category field, then press Ctrl+L

3 Click here

2 Double-click the class you want to apply

Using sub-classes

Applying a sub-class

Within the appropriate account, do the following:

REMEMBER

Quicken doesn't ship with preset classes or sub-classes – you have to create your own before you can use them.

(See the pages 48-49 for how to do this.)

REMEMBER

After step 2, press Ctrl+L. Then carry out steps 3-4.

1 Click in the relevant Category field

2 Type in a class, followed by :

4 Click here

3 Double-click the class you want to apply; Quicken applies it as a sub-class

Amending categories and classes

It's sometimes necessary to undertake category and class housekeeping. You can:

REMEMBER

When you revise a category or class, Quicken updates all associated transactions automatically.

- amend the category/class name

- alter (or add) associated descriptive text

- (in the case of categories) apply a different type

- transform categories into sub-categories (or vice versa)

Revising a category

Press Ctrl+C and carry out step 1 below, then steps 2-4 as appropriate. Finally, carry out step 5:

Click a category, then press Ctrl+E

HANDY TIP

To turn a category into a sub-category, highlight it in step 1. Then click this button and select a host category in the list.

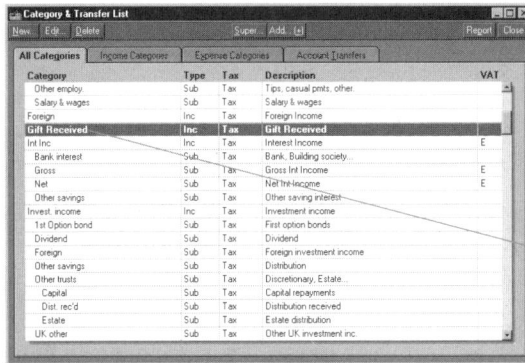

2 Rename the category

3 Revise/add descriptive text

HANDY TIP

To turn a sub-category into a category, highlight it in step 1. Then follow step 4.

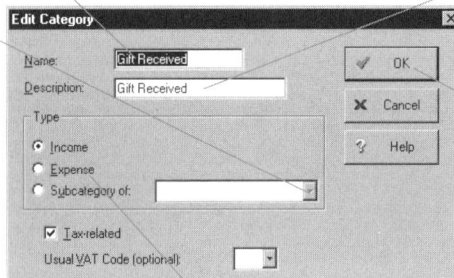

5 Click here

4 Click Income or Expense

Revising a class

Press Ctrl+L and do the following:

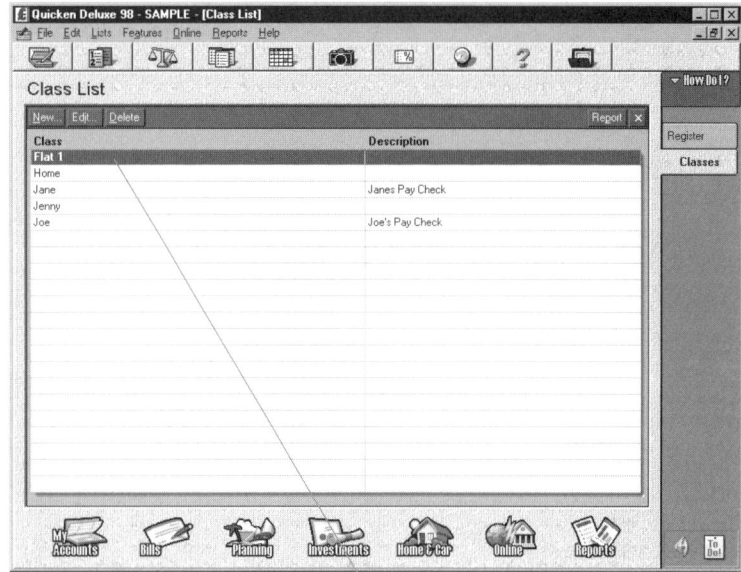

Click a class/sub-class

HANDY TIP **Since the only real difference between classes and sub-classes is the separating colon, you can change one into the other simply by altering the entry in the Category field within accounts:**

Category

2 Rename the class/sub-class

3 Optional – revise/ add descriptive text

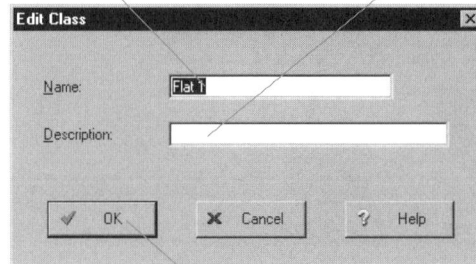

4 Click here

Deleting categories and classes

You can also delete categories and classes, as well as sub-categories and sub-classes. However, you should bear in mind the following:

- when you delete sub-categories and sub-classes, Quicken reallocates associated transactions to the parent category or class

- you can't delete a category which has one or more associated sub-categories. Instead, delete the sub-categories first and then the category

- you *can* delete a class which has associated sub-classes. This is because Quicken treats classes and sub-classes as fundamentally identical

Erasing classes and sub-classes

Press Ctrl+C or Ctrl+L to launch the Category & Transfer List or Class List dialogs respectively. Carry out step 1 below:

REMEMBER

After step 1, Quicken launches a special message. Click OK to proceed with the deletion.

Click here

Splits – an overview

So far, we've seen how categories and classes can be applied to transactions. This is more than sufficient for the majority of transactions, but consider the following situation.

A householder receives two premium requests from the same insurance company, at more or less the same time. Clearly, though, he won't want to write *two* separate cheques. Instead, he'll write one for the full amount, and this will appear in his Quicken account as a single transaction. However, it would help his accounts considerably if he could differentiate between the two amounts, since they are functionally distinct. In fact, he really has to do this to avoid the possibility of confusion in the future.

This sort of situation requires a special approach. Additional examples of situations which need this are:

- salary cheques, which can profitably be itemised to show the individual components

- self-employed writers receiving cheques which relate to multiple commissions

- transactions which relate to multiple payees

REMEMBER **Quicken comes with a preset category called 'Insurance', but no associated sub-categories. This example requires that you create your own sub-categories. (See pages 43-45 for how to do this.)**

Transaction splits

How does Quicken solve this problem? By allowing transactions to be 'split'. This is simply the process of applying multiple categories or classes to a single transaction. In general terms, and continuing our original example, you could split the joint insurance payment by applying two category/sub-category combinations:

Insurance:Home

Insurance:Car

to the overall amount. Each category/sub-category combination would have its share of the total premium allocated to it.

Creating splits

To apply a split, carry out the following steps (in the course of entering the appropriate transaction):

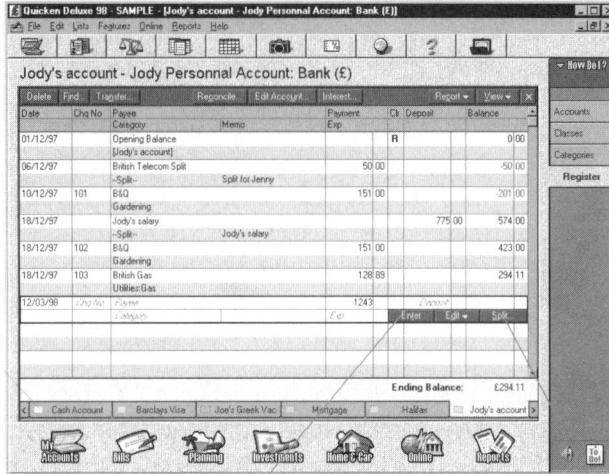

5 Click here

| Click here

HANDY TIP

Repeat steps 2 and 3 for as many components as you want to include in the split. Carry out step 4 when you've finished creating it.

REMEMBER

Quicken updates the balance here as you enter the split:

2 Apply or create the relevant category or class

3 Type in the amount for the split component

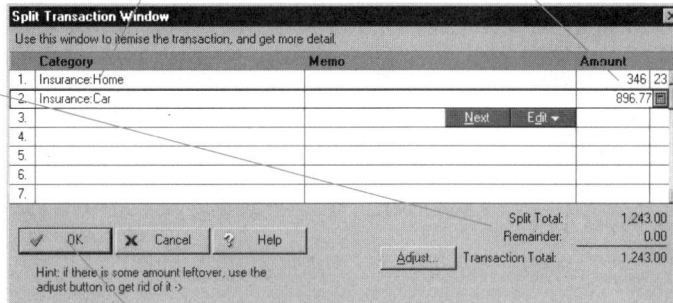

HANDY TIP

In this example, the transaction total is:
1243.00
split between two components of:
346.23
896.77

4 Click here

Revising splits - an overview

Revising splits which have already been set up – a task which is sometimes necessary – is a fairly straightforward job, but there are certain points you need to bear in mind:

HANDY TIP

Here, the first transaction split:

346.23

has been subtracted from the transaction total:

1243.00

and the difference:

896.77

inserted in the second split.

After you've entered a figure in the Amount field in the Splits dialog (step 3 on page 56):

Amount	
346	23
896	77

First split

Second split – see the HANDY TIP

Quicken subtracts this from the Register transaction total and inserts the remainder in the next free line.

So far, so good. However, if you do either of the following:

1.   alter the Register transaction total

2.   alter any of the individual splits

Quicken – unsurprisingly – registers a discrepancy. You need to tell it how to resolve it. You can do this by:

— (in the case of 1.) having Quicken allocate the discrepancy proportionately to the existing split items

REMEMBER

Sometimes the balancing split entry is a minus figure.

— (in the case of 2.) having Quicken adjust the transaction total in the Register in line with the discrepancy (this may involve deleting balancing split items – see page 58)

The ideal

You know you've successfully balanced a transaction and its splits when the Remainder field shows 0.00.

Split Total:	1,243.00
Remainder:	0.00
Transaction Total:	1,243.00

The sign of a correct split

Changing splits

REMEMBER

To adjust a split by revising the Register total, ignore steps 1-3. Instead, click in the Payment or Deposit fields and amend the relevant total. Follow step 4-6:

From within the relevant transaction, carry out the following steps to amend a split directly:

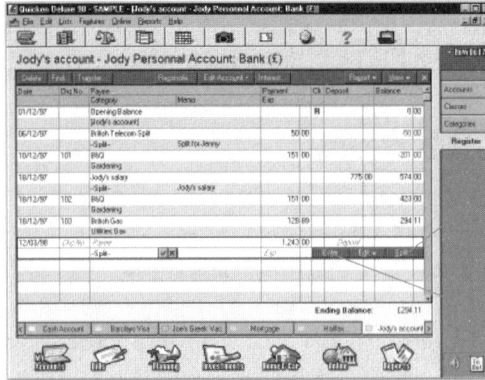

| Click here

6 Click here

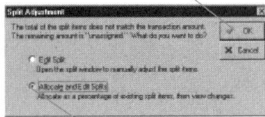

4 Click here

5 Select this

In the Split Transaction window, click OK.

2 Amend one or more split items

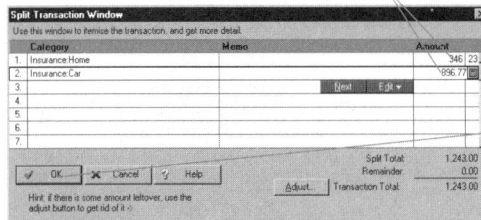

3 Click here to adjust the Register total

HANDY TIP

Re step 2 – if Quicken inserts a balancing split item, click the Adjust button to delete it and revise the Register total accordingly. Then follow steps 3-4.

Balancing split items

After step 2, Quicken may insert a balancing split item (if you've adjusted the final split item, AND the item total doesn't equal the Register total):

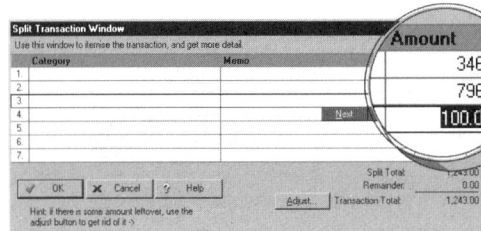

Balancing split item

See the HANDY TIP for how to deal with this.

Accounts

Use this chapter to learn how to create new accounts and open/amend existing ones. You'll also discover how to switch between accounts, and conceal accounts you don't want to acknowledge. Then you'll transfer money from one account to another, and delete/void specific transactions. Finally, you'll search for data within the Register, have it replaced automatically and print out your account details.

Chapter Three

Covers

Accounts – an overview

In Chapter 2, we looked at how to enter transactions into the account which was set up as part of the file – QDATA – created when you ran Quicken for the first time.

Some users find they only need this one account; others, on the other hand, discover that – as they become more proficient with Quicken – there is a need to create further accounts within the default file. This is a logical, and convenient progression. A common example would be the user who needs to utilise Quicken to manage his domestic affairs AND a small business. In this situation, having separate accounts for both makes a lot of sense. You don't *need* to do this (after all, you can use categories/sub-categories and/or classes/sub-classes to differentiate perfectly adequately between transaction types), but it is useful.

Quicken makes creating further accounts easy.

Other reasons for creating new accounts are:

- to handle individual businesses separately

- to handle petty cash transactions separately

- to track shares

- to track liabilities

- to track credit card debts

The last four examples involve Quicken account types which are beyond the scope of this book. However, the procedures for creating them are broadly identical with the standard account type.

Creating new accounts – method 1

There are three ways to create a new account.

Whichever method you use, the first requirement is to ensure that you've opened the correct Quicken file (see Chapter 1) *before* you begin to create your new account.

Using method 1

With the relevant file open, pull down the File menu and carry out the following steps:

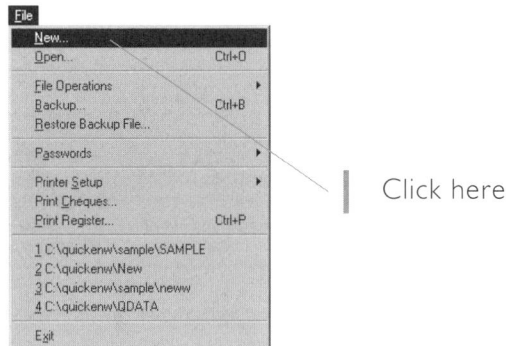

Click here

2 Click here

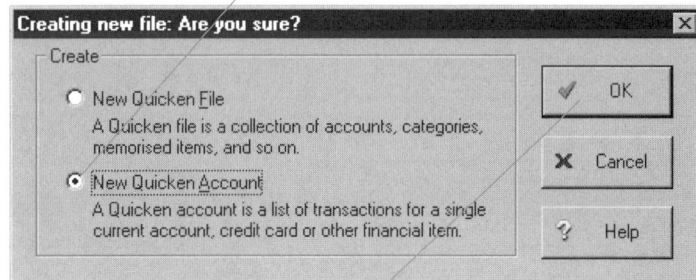

3 Click here

Now follow the additional steps on page 62.

Now perform the following additional steps:

4 Click an account type

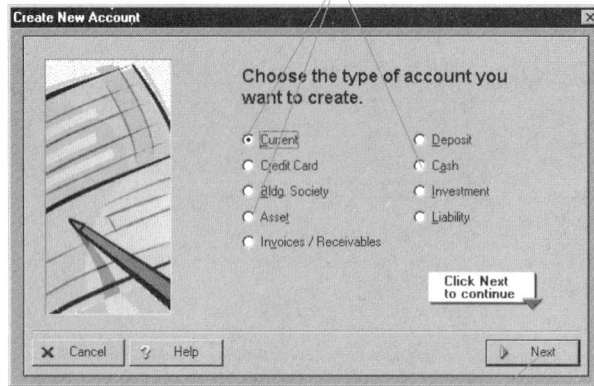

5 Click here

Quicken now launches a series of EasyStep dialogs (the first is shown below). Perform the following steps:

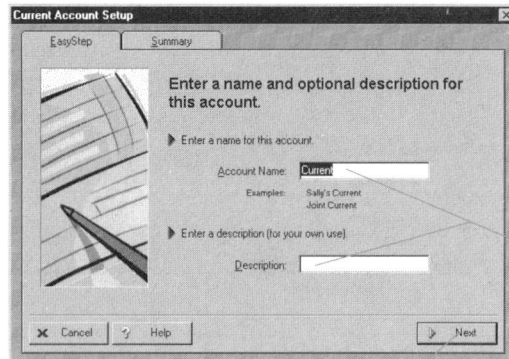

6 Complete these fields

7 Click here

...cont'd

Now perform the following additional steps:

Re step 8 – VAT tracking is beyond the scope of this book.

Quicken assumes you want to create a bank (current) account, since these are by far the most common. There are other types. Expertise you build up with bank accounts is to a large extent transferrable, since the account types work on very similar principles.

8 Click here

9 Click here

10 Click here; select a currency in the list

11 Click here

Carry out the following additional steps:

HANDY TIP

Re step 12 – if you don't have the last statement to hand:

- don't worry: the process of reconciliation (see Chapter 7) will resolve any disparity later

- note that the dialog shown below does not appear. Perform steps 12-13, but ignore 14-16. Then jump straight to page 65.

12 Make the appropriate choice

13 Click here

14 Type in the ending date

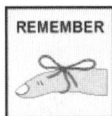

REMEMBER

The ending date is the date of your last statement; Quicken uses this as the inception date for your new account.
The ending balance is, in the case of bank accounts, the current balance.

15 Type in the ending balance

16 Click here

...cont'd

In the final stage, you confirm the information you've just entered.

REMEMBER

Check the information in these fields: correct any errors. **Finally, perform step 17.**

Do the following:

Current Account Setup

EazyStep | Summary

Account Information

Account Name: Current

Description:

Balance: 100.00   as of 18/03/98

Currency: Pound   ☐ Track VAT

Optional Information

Overdraft Limit, if Applicable:

Additional Information: Info...   Tax Info: Tax...

✕ Cancel   ? Help   ‹ Back   ✓ Done

17 Click here

This completes the process of creating your new account.

Current: Bank (£)

Delete | Find... | Transfer... | Reconcile... | Edit Account... | Interest... | Report ▾ | View ▾ | Close

Date	Chq No	Payee	Category	Payment	Clr	Deposit	Balance
18/03/98		Opening Balance	[Current]		R	100 00	100 00
18/03/98	Chq No	Payee	Category	Payment		Deposit	

Enter | Edit ▾ | Split

Ending Balance: £100.00

home | Mark P's Holiday... | Liability | VAT Control | Current

The new account

Creating new accounts – method 2

HANDY TIP

If you've created further Quicken files (see Chapter 1), make sure you've opened the correct one *before* you start to create a new account.

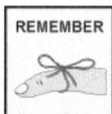

Using method 2

Do the following:

QuickTabs

REMEMBER

The Activity Bar can only be displayed if Quicken's QuickTabs are on-screen.

(See pages 13-14 for how to use QuickTabs).

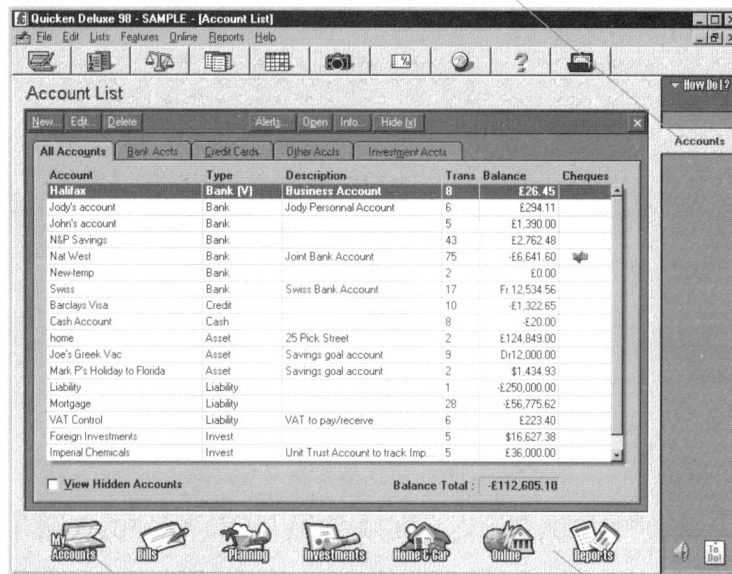

Place the mouse pointer here

The Activity Bar

My Accounts
Use My Register
▷ Create a New Account...
View My List of Accounts
Reconcile an Account
Estimate interest...
Set Up My Pay Cheque...
My net worth...

2 Click here

Now carry out steps 4-17, as appropriate, on pages 62-65.

Creating new accounts – method 3

Using method 3

Press Ctrl+A to launch the Account List. Now do the following:

REMEMBER **For more information on how to use the Account List, see page 68.**

1 Click here

2 Click an account type

3 Click here

Now carry out steps 6-17, as appropriate, on pages 62-65.

Opening accounts

After you've created an additional account, you need to open it in order to work with it.

You do this by using a special dialog – the Account List dialog. We've already seen how to use this to create new accounts (see page 67). However, you can use it to perform a variety of additional actions including:

- hiding inactive accounts

- account deletion

- editing accounts

Opening an account

Pull down the Lists menu and click Account. Now do the following:

(see page 67)

HANDY TIP **You can use a keyboard shortcut to launch the Account List dialog. Simply press Ctrl+A.**

2 Click here

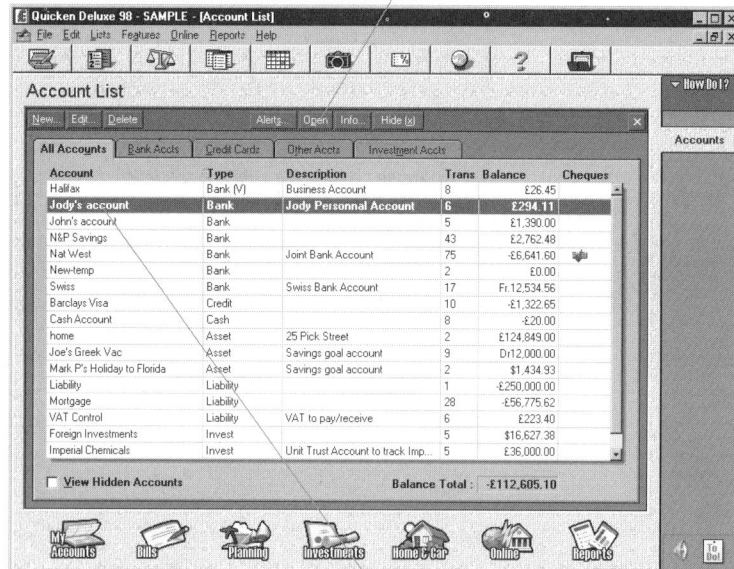

HANDY TIP **To close an account when you've finished using it, simply press Esc.**

Account	Type	Description	Trans	Balance	Cheques
Halifax	Bank (V)	Business Account	8	£26.45	
Jody's account	Bank	Jody Personnal Account	6	£294.11	
John's account	Bank		5	£1,390.00	
N&P Savings	Bank		43	£2,762.48	
Nat West	Bank	Joint Bank Account	75	-£6,641.60	
New-temp	Bank		2	£0.00	
Swiss	Bank	Swiss Bank Account	17	Fr.12,534.56	
Barclays Visa	Credit		10	-£1,322.65	
Cash Account	Cash		8	-£20.00	
home	Asset	25 Pick Street	2	£124,849.00	
Joe's Greek Vac	Asset	Savings goal account	9	Dr12,000.00	
Mark P's Holiday to Florida	Asset	Savings goal account	2	$1,434.93	
Liability	Liability		1	-£250,000.00	
Mortgage	Liability		28	-£56,775.62	
VAT Control	Liability	VAT to pay/receive	6	£223.40	
Foreign Investments	Invest		5	£16,627.38	
Imperial Chemicals	Invest	Unit Trust Account to track Imp...	5	£36,000.00	

Balance Total : -£112,605.10

Click the account
you want to open

Account navigation

After you've created additional accounts, you'll need to be able to move between them easily and conveniently. For this purpose, Quicken provides a special icon bar called the Account tab bar.

BEWARE

In Quicken, you can only open one account Register at a time.

Note that the Account tab bar appears irrespective of whether QuickTabs are displayed on-screen, and is therefore always available.

Using Account tabs

The Account tab bar is a special bar at the base of the account Register (and also at the bottom of the Write Cheque window – see Chapter 6) in which each account appears as an icon.

Ensure the Register is displayed (if it isn't, press Ctrl+R). Do the following:

Account tab bar

Date	Ref	Payee	Category	Decrease	Clr	Increase	Balance
13/01/97		Opening Balance	[Joe's Greek Vac]				0 00
13/03/97		Transfer for Holidat	[Nat West]			1,500 00	1,500 00
13/04/97		Transfer for Holidat	[Nat West]			1,500 00	3,000 00
13/05/97		Transfer for Holidat	[Nat West]			1,500 00	4,500 00
30/05/97		Transfer for Holidat	[Nat West]			1,500 00	6,000 00
13/06/97		Transfer for Holidat	[Nat West]			1,500 00	7,500 00
13/07/97		Transfer for Holidat	[Nat West]			1,500 00	9,000 00
13/08/97		Transfer for Holidat	[Nat West]			1,500 00	10,500 00
13/09/97		Transfer for Holidat	[Nat West]			1,500 00	12,000 00

Ending Balance: Dr12,000.00

Click the relevant icon
to jump to that account

Account editing – an overview

So far, we've looked at how to use the Account List dialog to:

- create new accounts

- open existing accounts

However, you can also use it to:

- amend account *details* (basic descriptive information relating to the way the account functions – for instance: the account name, the currency used and whether VAT tracking is in force)

- amend account *information* (optional additional information concerning the account – for instance, the name and phone number of the person you deal with, the account number and any supplementary comments you want to record)

- hide inactive accounts

- delete accounts

Remember that the process of deleting accounts is irreversible. The following actions happen when you proceed with a deletion:

1. all recorded transactions which relate to the deleted account are expunged from the host file and lost forever

2. all information relating to the account is destroyed

Because account deletions are permanent, Quicken launches a fail-safe procedure. A warning message appears before your instruction is complied with.

To proceed with the deletion, you have to type in 'yes' and click the appropriate button.

Editing accounts

Editing account details

Pull down the Lists menu and click Account. Now carry out the following steps:

2 Click here

HANDY TIP

Press Esc to close the Account List dialog when you've finished using it.

Click the account you want to edit

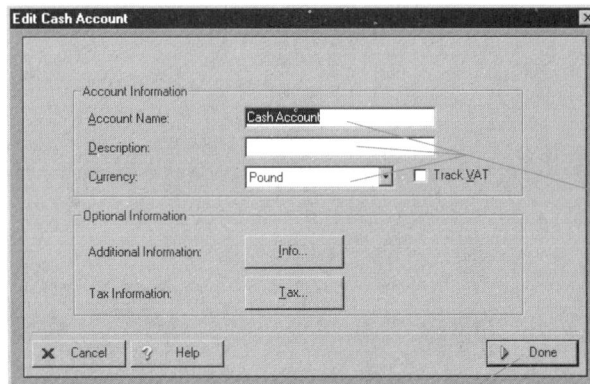

3 Make the necessary changes

4 Click here

Editing account information

Pull down the Lists menu and click Account. Now carry out the following steps:

HANDY TIP

Press Esc to close the Account List dialog when you've finished using it.

2 Click here

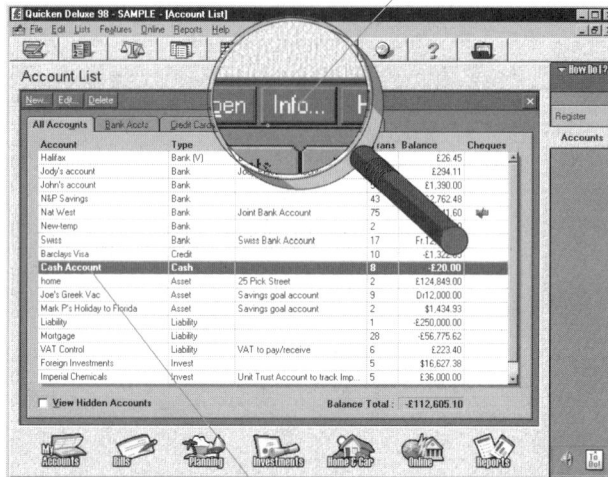

1 Click an account

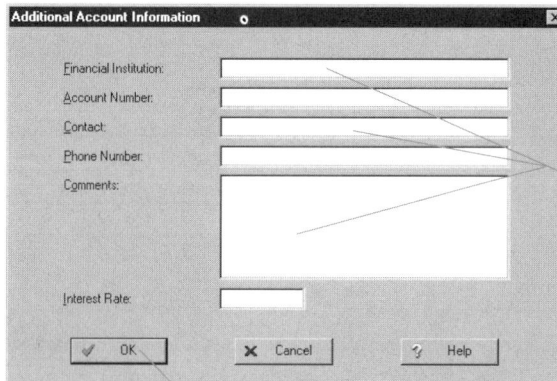

3 Make the necessary changes

4 Click here

Deleting accounts

Pull down the Lists menu and click Account. Now carry out the following steps:

2 Click here

HANDY TIP

Press Esc to close the Account List dialog when you've finished using it.

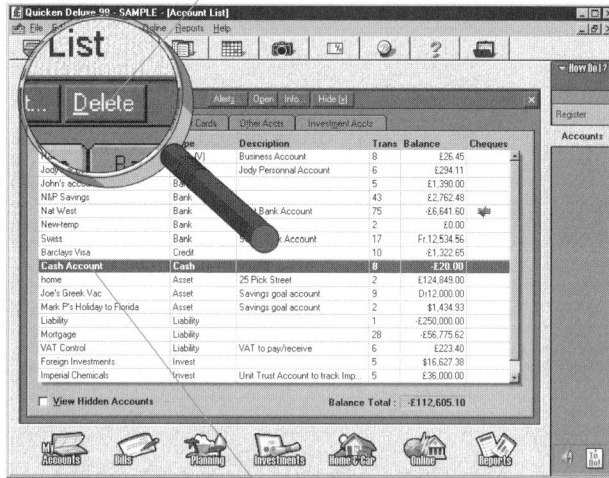

| Click an account

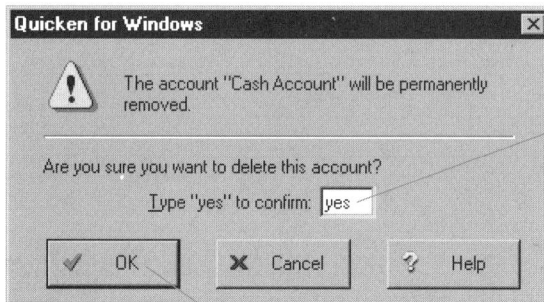

3 Type in 'yes' (but omit the quotes)

4 Click here

Hiding accounts

Quicken lets you 'hide' accounts. Accounts which are hidden:

- no longer appear in the Account List dialog

- are excluded from any graphs or reports you create

Hiding accounts is useful in certain situations, for instance:

— when the accounts concerned are obsolete

— when you want to see what your overall financial position looks like without taking one or more accounts into consideration

Hiding an account
Press Ctrl+A. Then do the following:

3 Click here

HANDY TIP

To view hidden accounts, make sure this *is* selected:

2 Click the account you want to hide

Ensure this isn't selected

HANDY TIP

To unconceal a hidden account, make sure View Hidden Accounts is selected. Then select it and repeat step 3.

Quicken 98 for Windows

This account will no longer be visible in the Account List. To view hidden accounts, select the 'View Hidden Accounts' checkbox at the bottom of the list.

✓ OK

4 Click here

Transferring money – an overview

There are situations when it becomes very useful to be able to transfer money from one Quicken account to another. Examples are:

- transferring money from a Building Society account to a Bank account (or vice versa)

- transferring money from a Bank account to a Credit Card account

Quicken makes this process very easy and straightforward. It does this by:

1. treating accounts as categories (for the purpose of internal transfers)

2. not making you enter transfers twice

These may require explanation.

Let's stipulate that you want to transfer money from a Building Society account into your current Bank account. Clearly, there are two inherent transactions here: the withdrawal out of your Building Society account, and the consequent deposit in your Bank account. Rather than have you insert both, Quicken lets you simply enter one in *either* account. When you enter it, you cross-refer it to the other account by applying a category which is simply the name of the other account. As long as you enter the details correctly (in particular, the deposit or withdrawal status), Quicken ties everything up automatically.

REMEMBER **Quicken stores account details as categories. However, it differentiates them from categories by enclosing them in square brackets.**

When you enter a transfer, you can combine it with a class (but not a category). For instance, if you're transferring money out of a Building Society account to pay the telephone bill, you might classify it as:

[Abbey National]/Telephone

Transferring money

To transfer money from one account to another, first create a new transaction in either of the accounts. Enter details in the normal way. Now do the following:

Click in the relevant Category field

REMEMBER

Account names are enclosed in square brackets:
[Jody's account]

3 Click here

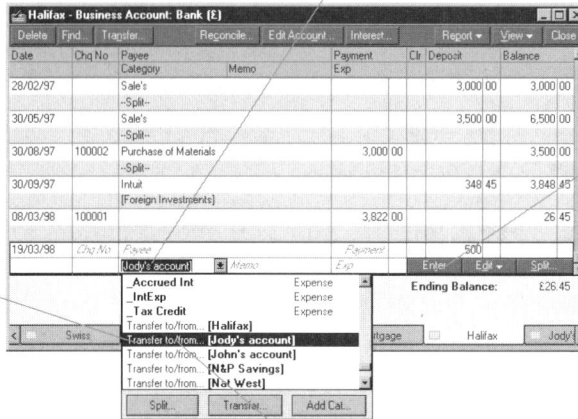

2 Click the second account

REMEMBER

This is the second account. Note the reference to the first account (magnified here for convenience):

The result of the transfer:

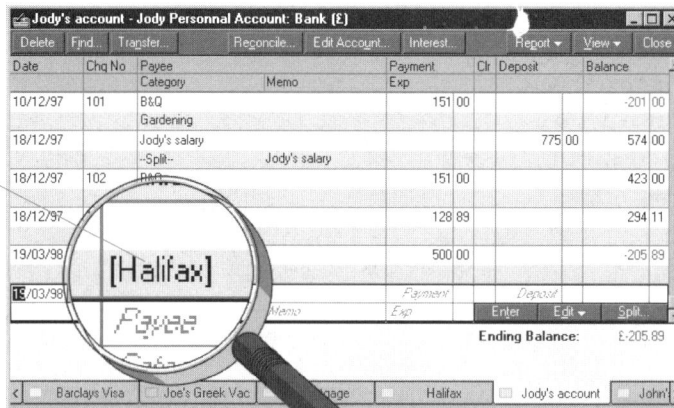

[Halifax]

Deleting and voiding – an overview

Sometimes it's necessary to delete or void transactions. However, it's important to be clear about the difference.

Deletion

Deleting a transaction erases it completely and permanently. Probably the only valid reason for deleting a transaction is if you've entered it into the wrong account.

Voiding

Voiding a transactions leaves it intact within the Register. However, its effect is nullified: it has no impact on the Ending Balance.

Voiding is considerably more useful than deletion. The classic situation where voiding is advisable is an incorrect cheque. It's necessary to stop it, clearly, but at the same time there is a need to retain an entry in the Register for future reference (principally for reconciliation purposes).

See the illustration below for an example of a voided transaction:

Magnified view of voided transaction

REMEMBER

Quicken inserts ****VOID**** **in the Payee field:**

Deleting transactions

Within the Register, do the following:

2 Click here

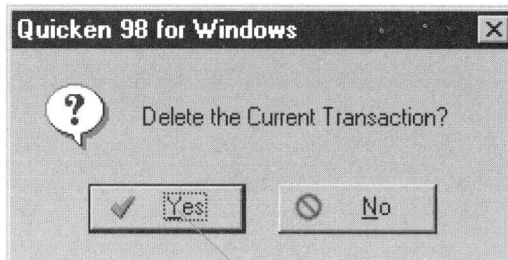

Nat West - Joint Bank Account: Bank (£)

Date	Chq No	Payee		Payment	Clr	Deposit	Balance
		Category	Memo	Exp			
03/01/98	TXFR	Transfer Money To Swiss Bank Account		100 00			-5,114 93
		[Swiss]					
12/01/98	Print	British Gas		128 89			-5,243 82
		Utilities:Gas					
28/01/98	Chq No	Halifax Property Ser,		470 00		Deposit	-5,713 82
		Rent Paid	Memo	Exp		Enter Edit Split	
03/02/98	TXFR	Transfer Money To Swiss Bank Account		100 00			-5,813 82
		[Swiss]					
12/02/98	Print	British Gas		128 89			-5,942 71
		Utilities:Gas					
28/02/98		Halifax Property Ser,		470 00			-6,412 71
		Rent Paid					
03/03/98	TXFR	Transfer Money To Swiss Bank Account		100 00			-6,512 71
		[Swiss]					
12/03/98	Print	British Gas		128 89			-6,641 60
		Utilities:Gas					
19/03/98							

Ending Balance: £-6,641.60

Nat West | N&P Savings | Swiss | Barclays Visa | Joe's Greek Vac | Mortgage

Click in the relevant transaction

Quicken 98 for Windows

? Delete the Current Transaction?

✓ Yes   ⊘ No

3 Click here

Voiding transactions

REMEMBER **After you've finished voiding the transaction, don't forget to click the Enter button.**

Within the Register, do the following:

Date	Chq No	Payee	Payment	Clr	Deposit	Balance
		Category	Exp			
03/01/98	TXFR	Transfer Money To Swiss Bank Account	100 00			-5,114 93
		[Swiss]				
12/01/98	Print	British Gas	128 89			-5,243 82
		Utilities:Gas				
28/01/98	*Chq No*	Halifax Property Ser,	470 00		*Deposit*	-5,713 82
		Rent Paid	*Exp*		*Enter Edit ▾ Split...*	
03/02/98	TXFR	Transfer Money To Swiss Bank Account	100 00			-5,813 82
		[Swiss]				
12/02/98	Print	British Gas	128 89			-5,942 71
		Utilities:Gas				
28/02/98		Halifax Property Ser,	470 00			-6,412 71
		Rent Paid				
03/03/98	TXFR	Transfer Money To Swiss Bank Account	100 00			-6,512 71
		[Swiss]				
12/03/98	Print	British Gas	128 89			-6,641 60
		Utilities:Gas				
19/03/98						

Nat West - Joint Bank Account: Bank (£)

Delete | Find... | Transfer... | Reconcile... | Edit Account... | Interest... | Report ▾ | View ▾ | Close

Ending Balance: £-6,641.60

☐ Nat West   ☐ N&P Savings   ☐ Swiss   ☐ Barclays Visa   ☐ Joe's Greek Vac   ☐ Mortgage

BEWARE **Voiding is immediate: there is no warning message first.**

Click in the relevant transaction

Now pull down the Edit menu and do the following:

2 Click here

Edit
Cut	Shift+Del
Copy	Ctrl+Ins
Paste	Shift+Ins
·Transaction ▸	
Find & Replace ▸	
Use Calculator...	
Options ▸	

Cut	
Copy	
Paste	
New	Ctrl+N
Delete	Ctrl+D
Insert	Ctrl+I
Void Transaction	Ctrl+V
Memorise	Ctrl+M
Restore	
Go To Transfer	Ctrl+X

3 Click here

Search operations

Locating specific transactions is easy when accounts are small. However, after you've been using Quicken for a while the number of transactions in any given account increases dramatically, and it becomes harder to find the one you want.

Quicken has a solution to this problem: its Find facility. You can search for numbers and/or text with just a few mouse clicks. For example, if you know a transaction has a Deposit entry of £652.15, you can search for this. Or if you're not sure of the precise amount, you can use wildcards.

**You can also have Quicken replace flagged data with information of your choice.
See page 83.**

HANDY TIP

Wildcards

You can also widen the scope of searches by applying wildcards (called 'match characters' in Quicken).

You can use any of the following, in any permutation:

?   stands for any single character

..   stands for any number of (unspecified) characters

~   tells Quicken to ignore matches for any following text

Some examples:

*   Searching for **6?** would find any transactions containing whole number values in the range **60** to **69**

*   On the other hand, **6..** would find *any* transaction hosting values whose first digit is **6** e.g. **6**, **652.15**, **6026.12** etc.

*   Searching for **~Rent Paid** in a Register containing transactions to which the Rent Paid category has been applied will not find those transactions (the ~ tells Quicken to flag only those transactions to which a different – or no – category has been applied)

Limiting the search

You can make search operations more precise by restricting them to:

HANDY TIP

You can combine field and match limitations, in a single search.

1.   a specific field

2.   a specific type of match

Quicken recognises a large number of match types. These are:

Exact	Will only locate precise matches
Starts With	Will only locate entries which begin with the specified text and/or numbers
Ends With	Will only locate entries which end with the specified text and/or numbers
Greater	Will only locate entries which contain numbers greater than the specified number
Greater or Equal	Will only locate entries which contain numbers greater than (or equal to) the specified number
Less	Will only locate entries which contain numbers less than the specified number
Less or Equal	Will only locate entries which contain numbers less than (or equal to) the specified number
Contains	Sets no specific match options

Running a search

From within the relevant account, pull down the Edit menu and click Find & Replace, Find. Now carry out step 1 below. To restrict the search, follow steps 2-3 and/or 4-5, as appropriate. Finally, carry out step 6 to have Quicken locate the first match in the Register, OR step 7 to have it compile a separate list of matches (see the HANDY TIP).

1 Type in search data

6 Click here

Quicken Find

Find: Magnet Restaurant

Search: All Fields

Match if: Contains

☑ Search Backwards

Find
Find All
Close
Help

2 Click here

4 Click here

7 Click here

Double-click the correct list entry; Quicken displays the transaction in the Register

All Fields
Amount
Cleared Status
Memo
Date
Category/Class
Cheque Number
Payee

3 Optional – restrict the search to a specific field

Contains
Exact
Starts With
Ends With
Greater
Greater or Equal
Less
Less or Equal

5 Apply a match type

Running a search-and-replace

From within the relevant account, pull down the Edit menu and carry out steps 1-2 below. Perform steps 3-4 (and see the HANDY TIP) to have Quicken compile a list of matching transactions. Then follow steps 5-7. Finally, carry out step 8 to initiate the substitution:

HANDY TIP

After step 3, use the Search and/or Match it fields to limit the substitution, as appropriate.
   Then carry out steps 4-8.

Click here

Edit

Cut	Shift+Del
Copy	Ctrl+Ins
Paste	Shift+Ins
Transaction	▶
Find & Replace	▶
Use Calculator...	
Options	▶

2 Click here

Find...	Ctrl+F
Find/Replace...	
Recategorise...	

REMEMBER

Re step 7 – when selected, a transaction has this:

✔

against it.

3 Type in search data

4 Click here

Find and Replace

Print...   Help   Close

Find:	Boots					Find All
Search:	All Fields	▼				Replace
Match it:	Contains	▼

| Replace: | Payee | ▼ |
| With: | Marks & Spencer | ▼ |

8 Click here

Date	Acct	Num	Payee	Cat	Memo	Clr	Amount
✔ 11/02/97	Nat ...	1240	Boots	Medical		R	-13.40
12/07/97	Barclay...		Boots	Medical			-11.95

☑ Show Matches in Split   Found in 2 Txns   Mark All   Clear All

REMEMBER

After step 8. Quicken launches a special message. Do the following:

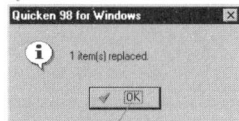

Quicken 98 for Windows

ⓘ 1 item(s) replaced

✔ OK

Click here

Finally, press Esc to close the Find and Replace dialog.

6 Type in the replacement data

7 Select one or more flagged transactions

5 Select the field in which the replacement should take place

Print options

Quicken lets you print out details of current transactions. You do this by printing the contents of the active account (but not the Register structure itself). You can also print category lists and class lists. This is a useful feature. When the number of categories or classes you use is large, it can sometimes be preferable to refer to a printed list to find the one you want to use than to scroll through the on-screen Category drop-down list.

REMEMBER

Before you start printing, ensure the correct printer is selected – for how to do this, see your Windows documentation.

Printing the Register contents

Pull down the File menu and click Print Register. Do the following:

Optional – name the print-out

2 Enter start and end dates, if appropriate

3 Click here to begin the print run

Printing lists

Pull down the Lists menu and click Category & Transfer or Class, as appropriate. Press Ctrl+P. Now do the following:

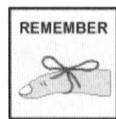

Click an orientation

REMEMBER

Ensure your printer is selected:

3 Click here to begin printing

2 Optional – to print only specific pages, enter start & end numbers

Memorising Transactions

Use this chapter to save time and effort by memorising frequently used transactions (automatically or manually) for easy insertion later. You'll also learn more about another time- and labour-saving aid: QuickFill.

Covers

Chapter Four

Memorisation – an overview

In Chapter 2, we took a brief look at the use of QuickFill to speed up data entry. To recap, when you click in certain fields, a boxed arrow appears; clicking this produces a drop-down list of available options. This is useful (and we'll discuss it in more depth later), but QuickFill offers more.

Most Quicken users find that they enter the same transaction – with the same payee and amount entries – time after time. A prime example of this would be a standing order; in essence, only the date of each payment alters. QuickFill helps you with repetitive transactions like this by automatically memorising details. Once a transaction has been committed to QuickFill's internal list of memorised transactions, all you have to do to invoke it is type in the first few characters of the payee's name.

(See pages 96-98 for information on additional uses of QuickFill to automate account procedures.)

The illustration below shows the result of clicking the boxed arrow to the right of a transaction's Payee field when automatic memorisation is in force:

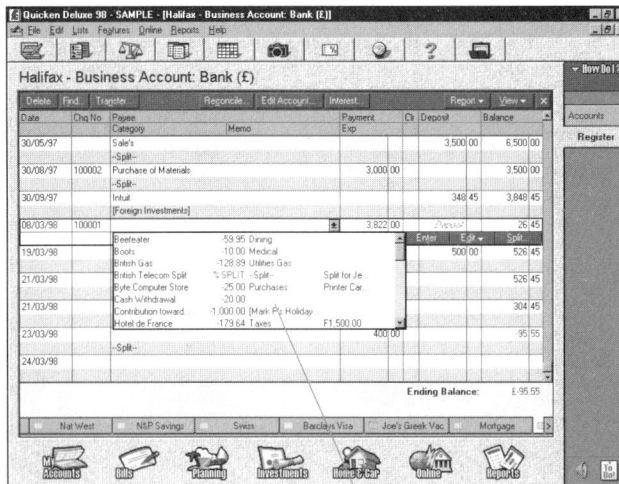

> **HANDY TIP**
>
> **Most users have transactions memorised automatically. However, you can memorise them manually, if you prefer.**
>   **See pages 88-91 for how to do this.**

The list of available transactions

Automatic memorisation

To turn automatic memorisation on or off, pull down the Edit menu and do the following:

1 Click here

Edit

Cut	Shift+Del
Copy	Ctrl+Ins
Paste	Shift+Ins
Transaction	▶
Find & Replace	▶
Use Calculator...	
Options	▶

Quicken Program...
Register...
Write Cheques...
Reports...
Graphs...

Reminders...
Internet Connection...
Desktop...
Iconbar...
International...

2 Click here

HANDY TIP

Re step 4 – the ✔ means that automatic memorisation is currently active.

3 Click this tab

Register Options

Display	Miscellaneous	QuickFill

Data Entry
- ☐ Use Enter Key to Move Between Fields
- ☑ Complete Fields Using Previous Entries
- ☑ Recall Memorised Transactions (requires auto-completion)
- ☑ Drop Down Lists on Field Entry
- ☑ Auto-Capitalise Payees & Categories

Automatic List Updating
- ☑ Auto Memorise New Transactions
- ☑ Auto Memorise to the Calendar List

✔ OK
✘ Cancel
? Help

5 Click here

REMEMBER

For details of how to use other options shown in this dialog, see pages 96-98.

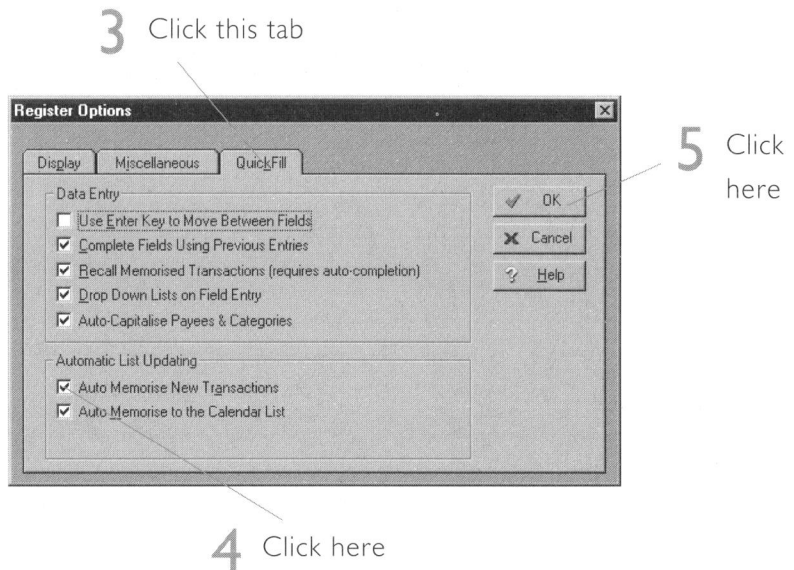

4 Click here

Manual memorisation

If you don't enter many transactions into your account(s), it may pay you to ensure automatic memorisation is turned off – see page 87 for how to do this. In this situation, you can simply memorise any transaction you're likely to need on an ad hoc basis.

You can:

- memorise transactions manually from within the Register, either on-the-fly or after you've recorded them

- memorise transactions manually from within a special dialog

REMEMBER

If you memorise a transaction on-the-fly, from within the Register (the quickest and most convenient method), you should only complete those fields you want to memorise.

Memorising a transaction from the Register

If you want to memorise a transaction you've already entered, carry out step 2 below. Alternatively, to memorise a transaction while you're in the process of entering it, follow step 1.

Complete the relevant fields

2 Click in the relevant transaction

Now pull down the Edit menu and do the following:

3 Click here

You can use a keyboard shortcut here. **Simply press Ctrl+M instead of carrying out steps 3-4.**

Edit	
Cut	Shift+Del
Copy	Ctrl+Ins
Paste	Shift+Ins
Transaction	▶
Find & Replace	▶
Use Calculator...	
Options	▶

Cut	
Copy	
Paste	
New	Ctrl+N
Delete	Ctrl+D
Insert	Ctrl+I
Void Transaction	Ctrl+V
Memorise	Ctrl+M
Restore	
Go To Transfer	Ctrl+X

4 Click here

Quicken 98 for Windows

This transaction is about to be memorised.

✓ OK   ✗ Cancel

5 Click here

Memorising a transaction outside the Register

Pull down the Lists menu and do the following:

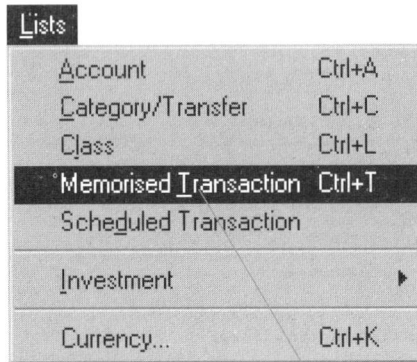

**You can use a keyboard shortcut to launch the Memorised Transaction List dialog.
Simply press Ctrl+T instead of performing step 1.**

HANDY TIP

| Click here

2 Click here

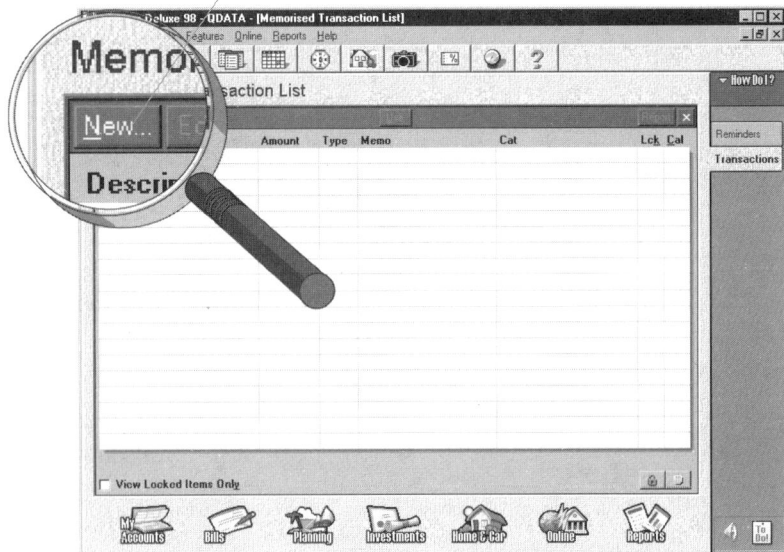

...cont'd

Now carry out step 3 below. If applicable, follow step 4.
Finally, carry out step 5:

3 Click here; select a
   transaction type in the list

5 Click
  here

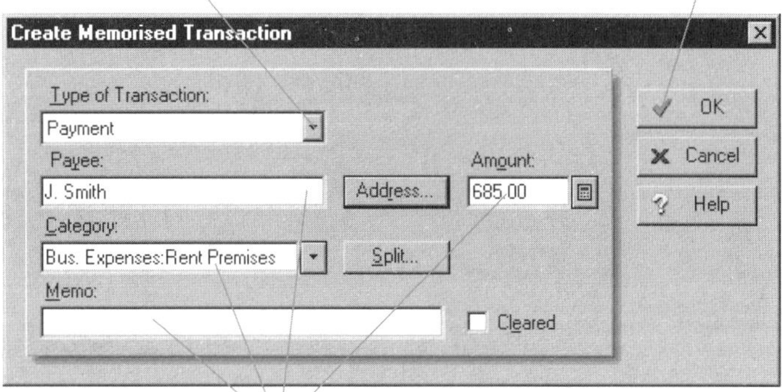

4 Complete these as necessary

The result:

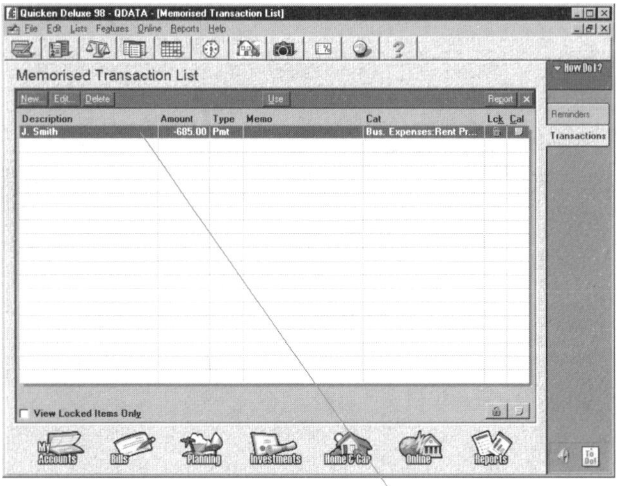

The new memorised transaction

Using memorised transactions

We've already seen how the Memorised Transaction List dialog can be used to create new memorised transactions. However, it can also be used to:

- insert a transaction you've already memorised into an account

- delete a memorised transaction (but only its entry in the Memorised Transaction List dialog, NOT where it's been used in the Register)

- revise the details of memorised transactions

Inserting a memorised transaction

Within the active account, do the following:

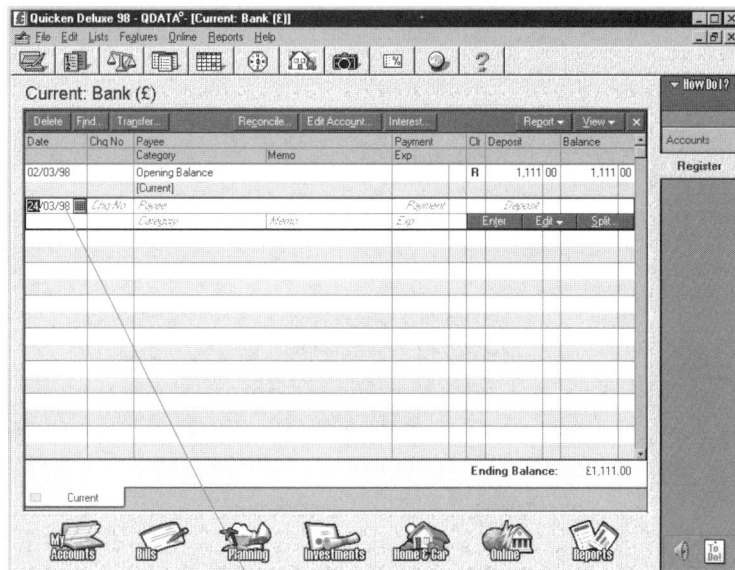

Click in a new transaction

Pull down the Lists menu and click Memorised
Transaction. Now carry out the following additional steps:

3 Click here

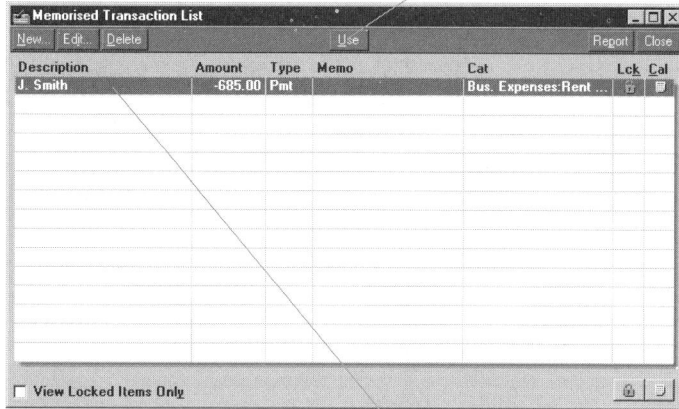

2 Select a memorised transaction

The illustration below shows the original account after
steps 1-3 have been carried out:

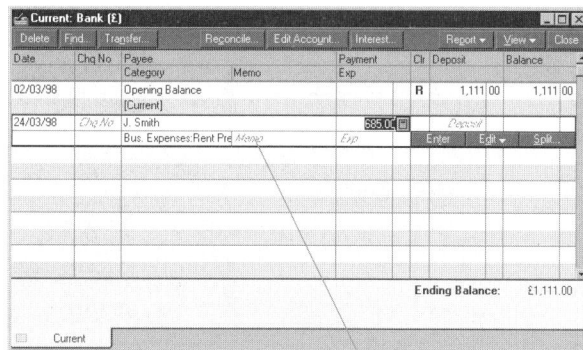

The inserted transaction

Revising memorised transactions

To amend a memorised transaction you've already set up, pull down the Lists menu and click Memorised Transaction. Now carry out the following steps:

2 Click here

Memorised Transaction List					
New..	Edit..	Delete		Use	Report Close

Description	Amount	Type	Memo	Cat	Lck Cal
J. Smith	-685.00	Pmt		Bus. Expenses:Rent ...	

☐ View Locked Items Only

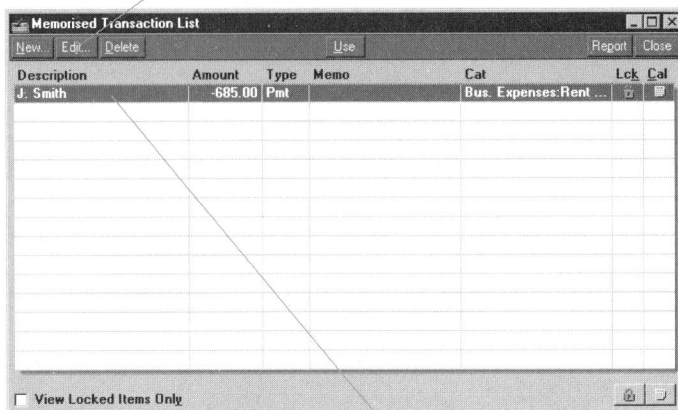

| Select a memorised transaction

4 Click here

Create Memorised Transaction

Type of Transaction:
Payment

Payee: J. Smith   Address...   Amount: 685.00

Category: Bus. Expenses:Rent Premises   Split...

Memo: ☐ Cleared

✔ OK
✘ Cancel
Help

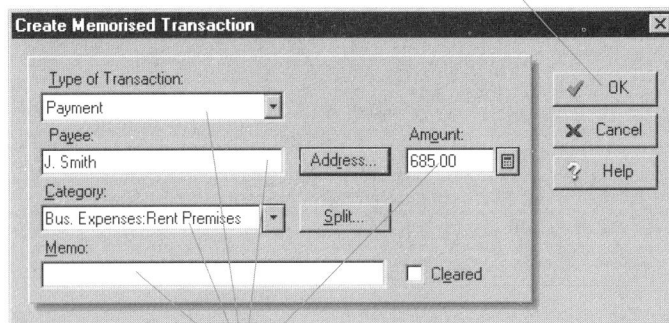

3 Amend these as necessary

Deleting memorised transactions

To delete a memorised transaction you've previously set up, pull down the Lists menu and click Memorised Transaction. Now carry out the following steps:

2 Click here

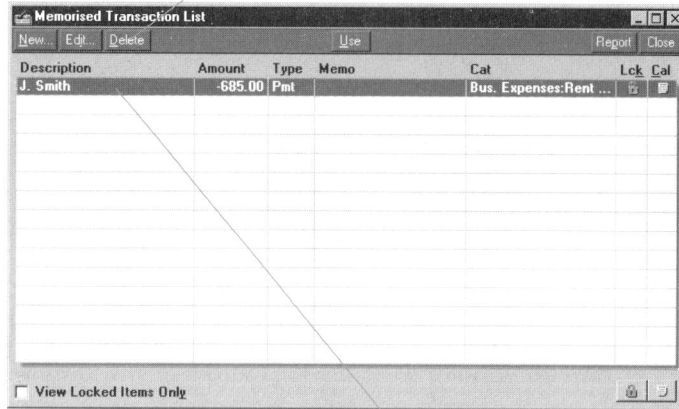

Select a memorised transaction

Quicken now launches a warning message. Carry out step 3 below:

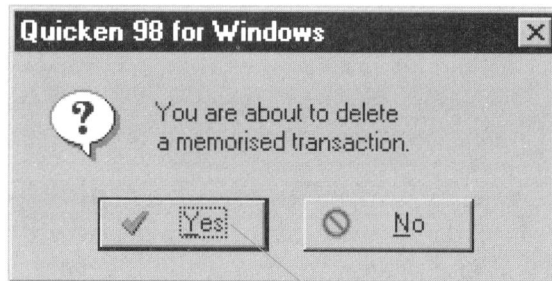

3 Click here

QuickFill – an overview

We saw earlier how QuickFill can be used to memorise transactions automatically. This is a useful device for Quicken users who enter a lot of transactions. However, QuickFill offers these additional options:

1. Complete Fields Using Previous Entries

HANDY TIP

If the proffered choice isn't right, you can continue typing data until it is.

When it is right, press Tab or Enter to confirm insertion of the data.

When this is active, typing in the first few characters in most fields prompts Quicken to display any matches. For example, typing in 'U' in the Category field of a new transaction produces:

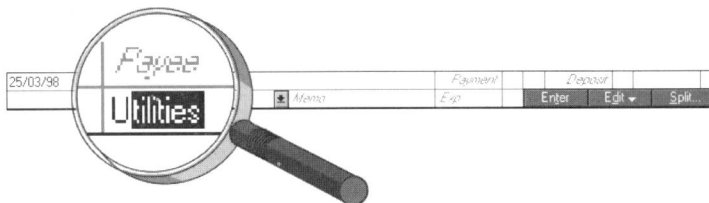

In this case, QuickFill assumes you want to insert Utilities and inserts it.

2. Recall Memorized Transactions

REMEMBER

You should note that the 'Recall Memorized Transactions' option is only available if the following feature has been selected: Complete Fields Using Previous Entries

This QuickFill option only works with the Payee field. If you begin to type in payee details, QuickFill responds by inserting the entire transaction (irrespective of whether it has been memorised or not – the only proviso is that you must have entered it previously).

3. Drop Down Lists on Field Entry

This option ensures that, whenever you click in any field – or move to it by pressing Tab as often as necessary – Quicken launches a drop-down list of available options.

4. Show Buttons on QuickFill Fields

This option displays a boxed arrow to the right of most fields when you place the insertion point in them:

Clicking on the arrow produces a list of memorised options; click the one you want to use.

Using QuickFill

Activating options 1-3 on page 96

Pull down the Edit menu and carry out the following steps:

HANDY TIP To deactivate any of these options, simply repeat steps 1-5, as appropriate.

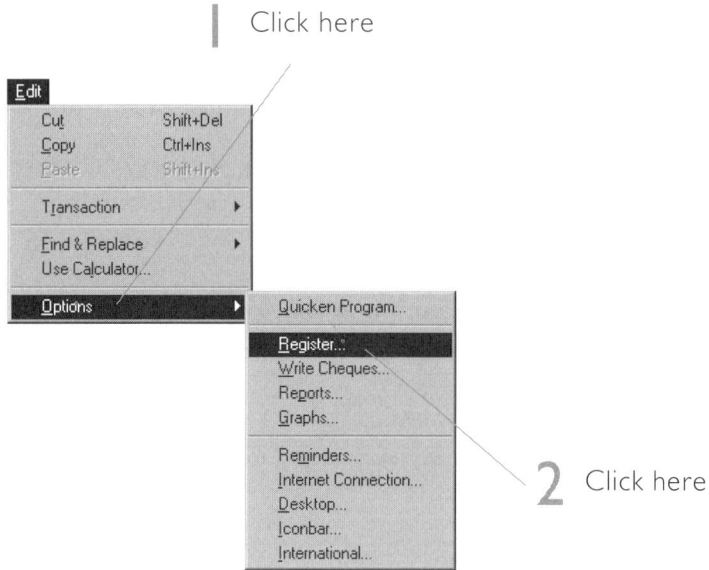

1 Click here

Edit

Cut	Shift+Del
Copy	Ctrl+Ins
Paste	Shift+Ins
Transaction	▶
Find & Replace	▶
Use Calculator...	
Options	▶

Quicken Program...

Register...
Write Cheques...
Reports...
Graphs...

Reminders...
Internet Connection...
Desktop...
Iconbar...
International...

2 Click here

3 Ensure this tab is active

Register Options.   ✕

Display	Miscellaneous	QuickFill

Data Entry
- ☐ Use Enter Key to Move Between Fields
- ☑ Complete Fields Using Previous Entries
- ☐ Recall Memorised Transactions (requires auto-completion)
- ☑ Drop Down Lists on Field Entry
- ☑ Auto-Capitalise Payees & Categories

Automatic List Updating
- ☑ Auto Memorise New Transactions
- ☑ Auto Memorise to the Calendar List

✔ OK
✖ Cancel
❓ Help

HANDY TIP Re step 4 – ✔ against an option means that it's currently active.

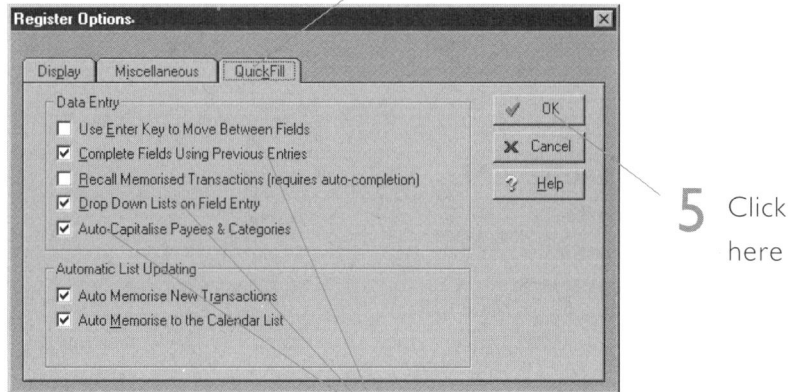

5 Click here

4 Click one or more options

...cont'd

Activating option 4 on page 96
Pull down the Edit menu and carry out the following steps:

Click here

Edit	
Cut	Shift+Del
Copy	Ctrl+Ins
Paste	Shift+Ins
Transaction	▶
Find & Replace	▶
Use Calculator...	
Options	▶

Quicken Program...
Register...
Write Cheques...
Reports...
Graphs...
Reminders...
Internet Connection...
Desktop...
Iconbar...
International...

HANDY TIP **To deactivate any of these options, simply repeat steps 1-5, as appropriate.**

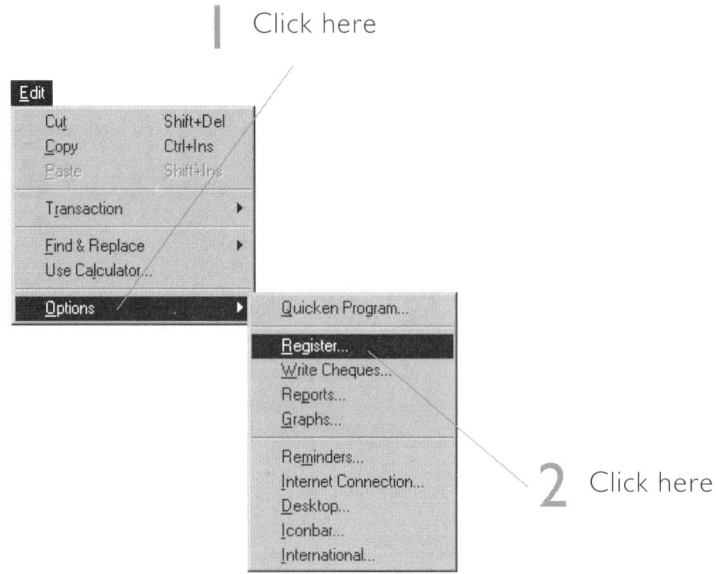

2 Click here

3 Ensure this tab is active

Register Options ✕

Display	Miscellaneous	QuickFill

Register Fields
☑ Show Date In First Column
☐ Show Memo before Category
☑ Show Buttons on QuickFill Fields

Register Appearance
☑ Use Colour Shading
☑ Show Transaction Toolbar
☑ Use One Cheque Register Window

Fonts...
Colours...

✓ OK
✕ Cancel
? Help

HANDY TIP **Re step 4 – ✔ against an option means that it's currently active.**

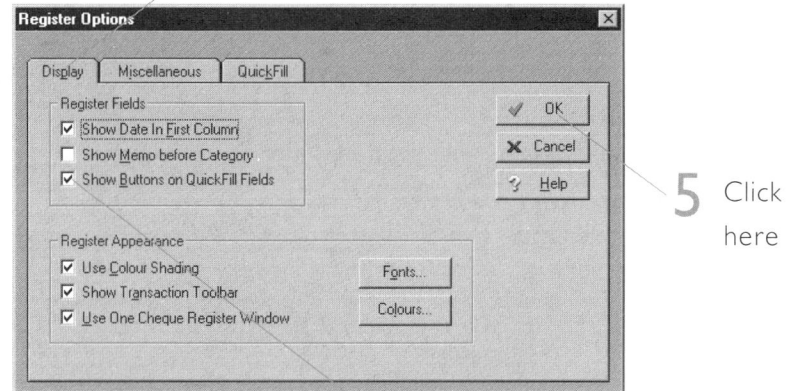

5 Click here

4 Click here

Standing Orders

Use this chapter to learn how to set up standing orders and direct debits in your accounts. Once you've set them up, you can fine-tune them as necessary, modifying their details or suspending them. You'll also discover how to save time and effort by creating, inserting and modifying transaction groups (logical associations of transactions which fall due around the same time). Also covered are standing order and transaction group housekeeping.

Covers

Chapter Five

Standing orders – an overview

Standing orders transfer *fixed* amounts out of your bank account at regular intervals, while direct debits perform the same function with *variable* amounts.

Quicken makes it easy to include standing orders and direct debits in your accounts. You can:

- choose not to specify transaction amounts for direct debits (because they fluctuate)

- restrict the number of payments

- backdate standing order or direct debit payments (to allow for payments already made)

- postdate standing order or direct debit payments (e.g. to allow time for cheque writing and submission)

- have standing order and direct debit transactions entered into your accounts automatically (or subject to manual confirmation)

- be very precise about which accounts standing order and direct debit transactions are taken from

REMEMBER

This is an example of a standing order inserted into an account. Notice that it looks just like a standard transaction:

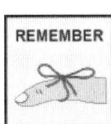

Quicken provides a special dialog – the Create Scheduled Transaction List/Standing Order List dialog – from which you can set up standing orders and direct debits. You can:

- specify the account into which you want a standing order/direct debit inserted

- specify a payment date

- apply any of the following to the standing order/direct debit:

  — payee details

  — brief descriptive text

  — a category/sub-category combination

- specify the payment amount (in the case of standing orders only)

- stipulate a payment frequency – normally monthly, but other options are:

  — only once

  — weekly

  — every two weeks

  — twice a month

  — every four weeks

  — every two months

  — quarterly

  — twice a year

  — yearly

- specify the number of payments

REMEMBER

By default, Quicken inserts the number of payments as 999 (i.e. infinite). Only change this if you want to specify a precise total.

Entering standing orders – method 1

To enter a standing order or direct debit, pull down the Lists menu and carry out the following steps:

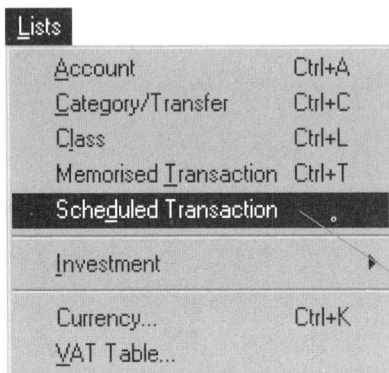

Click here

HANDY TIP

You can also use Quicken's Financial Calendar to insert standing orders and direct debits – see page 104.

2 Click here

Now carry out step 3 below. To select an account, follow steps 4-5. To select an entry method, carry out 6-7. To assign a frequency, follow step 8. To specify a payment number, carry out step 9. To postdate payment, follow step 10. Finally carry out step 11.

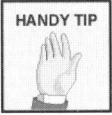

HANDY TIP

Before you carry out step 11, complete the fields in this section of the dialog, as appropriate:

In particular, insert the amount of the payment in the Amount field:

35.00

4 Click here

3 Type in a payment date

Create Scheduled Transaction / Standing Order

Account to use: John's account
Type of Transaction: Payment

✓ OK
✗ Cancel
? Help

Payee: British Gas
Address...
Next Date: 25/03/98

Category: Utilities:Gas
Split...
Amount: 35.00

Group

Num Field:

Memo:

☐ Irregular First Payment Amount

How Often: Monthly

Number of Payments (999 = indefinitely): 999

Record in Register: Prompt before enter

Record This Many Days In Advance: 0

11 Click here

9 Type in a payment no.

10 Type in a postdate no.

REMEMBER

Re step 10 – enter a value here to have Quicken postdate the transaction (i.e. enter it in advance of when the payment is due).

Note, however, that the payment effective date is unaltered.

6 Click here

8 Click here; select a frequency in the list

Halifax
Jody's account
John's account
N&P Savings
Nat West
New-temp

5 Click an account

Automatically enter
Prompt before enter

7 Click an entry method

Entering standing orders – method 2

HANDY TIP

See
Chapter 9
for more
information
on using the
Financial Calendar.

You can also use another method to enter standing orders/ direct debits: Quicken's Financial Calendar. Refer to the overhead Iconbar and do the following:

Click here

HANDY TIP

Use these
buttons:
to jump to
a different
month.

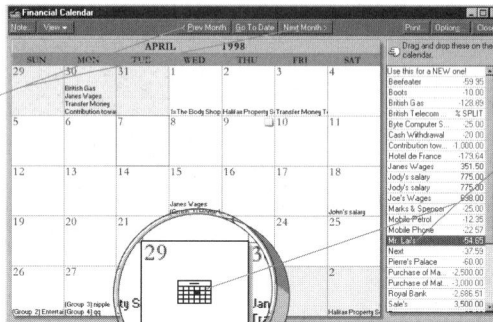

2 Click a
transaction in
the list; drag it
to the relevant
date

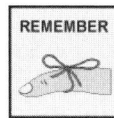

REMEMBER

The
Calendar
icon:
signifies
that you're about to
insert a transaction.

3 Click here; select an
account in the list

4 Click here; select a
payment type in the list

HANDY TIP

Ensure
Scheduled
Transaction
is active:

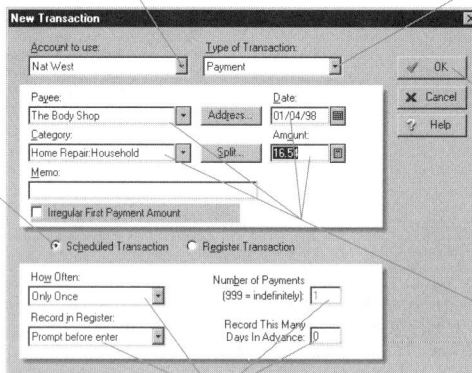

7 Click here

REMEMBER

See page
103 for
more
information
on how to complete
the fields in this
dialog.

5 Complete these
fields

6 Complete these fields

Revising standing orders

Standing orders and direct debits you've already set up sometimes require housekeeping. This can take the following forms:

• modifying standing order and direct debit settings and parameters

• forcing Quicken to pay a standing order or direct debit instalment immediately, even if – technically – it isn't yet due

• deleting a standing order/direct debit when it's run its course

• deactivating a standing order/direct debit when it's run its course

Deletion/deactivation

It's important to be clear in your mind about the distinction between *deletion* and *deactivation*.

Deleting a standing order/direct debit erases it irrevocably. This is the correct course if the standing order/direct debit relates to items which have now been paid in full. If this isn't the case, however, use deactivation. Deactivation suspends a standing order/direct debit by instructing Quicken not to enter any more payments, leaving its entry in the Scheduled Transaction/Standing Order List dialog (see the excerpt below) intact.

HANDY TIP **Standing orders and direct debits which have been deactivated can easily be reactivated, if the need arises. (See page 110 for how to do this).**

'None' in the Next Date field means the standing order or direct debit has been deactivated

Revising a standing order/direct debit

Pull down the Lists menu and carry out the following steps:

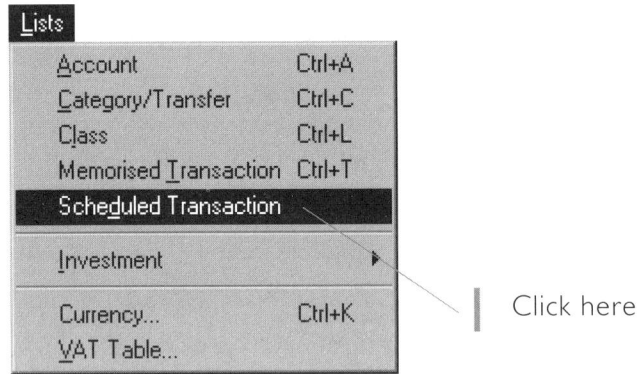

Click here

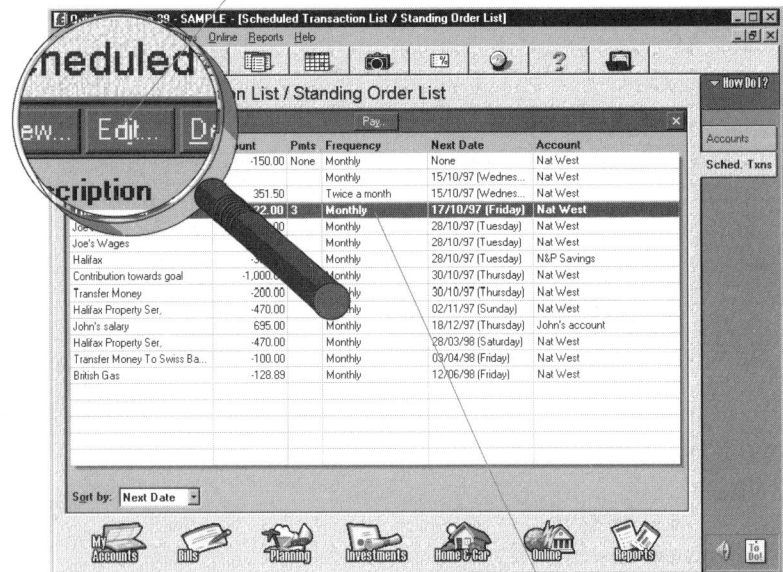

3 Click here

2 Click a standing order/direct debit

...cont'd

To continue amending the standing order/direct debit, carry out step 4 below. To select an alternative account, follow steps 5-6. To select an alternative entry method, carry out 7-8. To assign a new frequency, follow step 9. To specify a new payment number, carry out step 10. To postdate payment, follow step 11. Finally carry out step 12.

HANDY TIP

Before you carry out step 12, complete the fields in this section of the dialog, as appropriate:
In particular, insert the amount of the payment in the Amount field:

128.89

5 Click here

4 Type in a payment date

12 Click here

10 Enter a payment no.

11 Enter a postdate no.

REMEMBER

Re step 11 – any value in this field specifies the interval (in days) between Quicken's recording of the transaction and when it's due.
Note, however, that the payment effective date is unaltered.

7 Click here

9 Click here; select a frequency in the list

John's account
N&P Savings
Nat West
New-temp
Swiss
Barclays Visa

6 Click an account

Automatically enter
Prompt before enter

8 Click an entry method

Forcing payment of standing orders

To have Quicken pay standing orders or direct debits, pull down the Lists menu and click Scheduled Transaction. Now carry out the following steps:

2 Click here

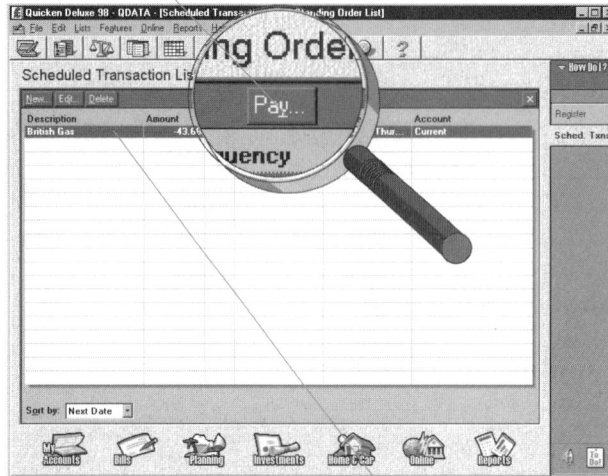

Click a standing order/direct debit

3 Click here

Deleting standing orders

To delete standing orders and direct debits, pull down the Lists menu and carry out the following steps:

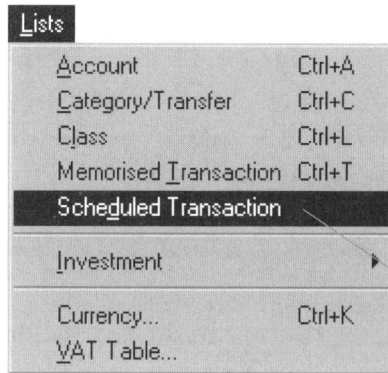

Lists

Account	Ctrl+A
Category/Transfer	Ctrl+C
Class	Ctrl+L
Memorised Transaction	Ctrl+T
Scheduled Transaction	
Investment	▶
Currency...	Ctrl+K
VAT Table...	

| Click here

3 Click here

REMEMBER

After step 3, Quicken launches a special warning message. Do the following:

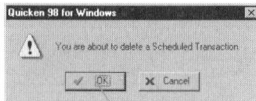

Quicken 98 for Windows

⚠ You are about to delete a Scheduled Transaction

✓ OK   ✗ Cancel

Click here to proceed with the deletion

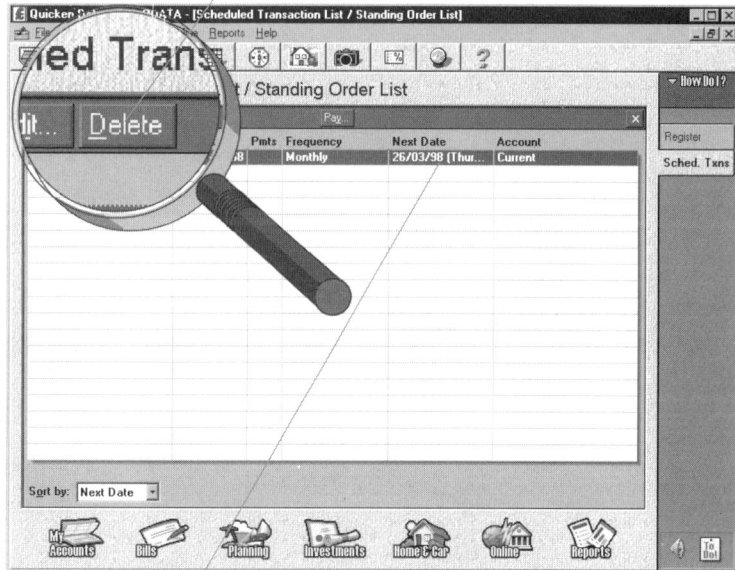

Quicken ... DATA - [Scheduled Transaction List / Standing Order List]

ed Trans ... t / Standing Order List

Pay

|it... | Delete |

	Pmts	Frequency	Next Date	Account
8		Monthly	26/03/98 [Thur...	Current

How Do I?

Register

Sched. Txns

Sort by: Next Date

My Accounts   Bills   Planning   Investments   Home & Car   Online   Reports

2 Click a standing order/direct debit

Deactivating standing orders

To deactivate a standing order/direct debit, pull down the Lists menu and click Scheduled Transaction. Now carry out the following steps:

2 Click here

Click a standing order/direct debit

HANDY TIP **If you need to reactivate a standing order/direct debit, simply type in a positive number here:**

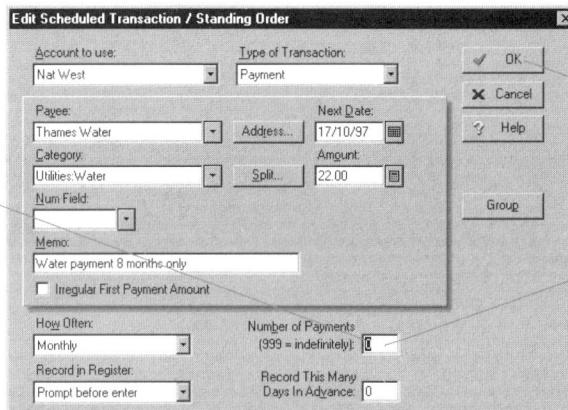

4 Click here

3 Type in 0 (zero) here

Transaction groups – an overview

Quicken provides another time- and labour-saving aid: it lets you organise transactions into convenient 'transaction groups'.

Transaction groups are logical associations of transactions (deposits or withdrawals, but more usually withdrawals) which fall due around the same time. The individual transactions need have nothing in common apart from:

- the date on which they fall due

- the fact that they have all been memorised (note that you can only include memorised transactions in a transaction group)

When you set up a transaction group:

- you allocate an overall name to it. This means that – where applicable – multiple transactions can be dealt with as one entity

- Quicken provides a reminder when the date on which the constituent transactions fall due approaches

- all the individual transactions are entered at once if you tell Quicken to action the group

In this way, transaction groups act as a reminder system.

You can set up as many as 12 transaction groups within a given account.

A transaction group, listed in the Scheduled Transaction List dialog

Setting up a transaction group

Pull down the Lists menu and do the following:

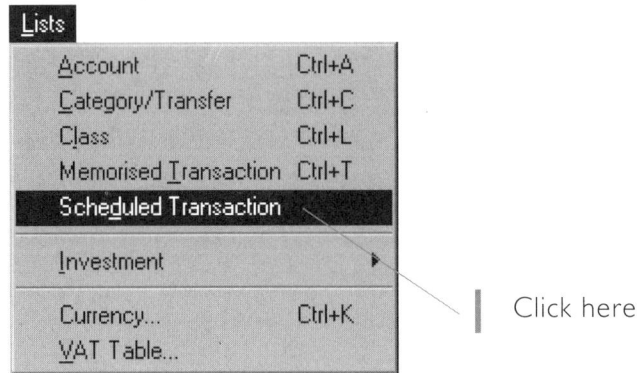

Lists

Account	Ctrl+A
Category/Transfer	Ctrl+C
Class	Ctrl+L
Memorised Transaction	Ctrl+T
Scheduled Transaction	
Investment	▶
Currency...	Ctrl+K
VAT Table...	

Click here

2 Click here

Deluxe 98 - QDATA - [Scheduled Transaction List / Standing Order List]

Features Online Reports Help

Sched...   ...action List / Standing Order List

New...

Amount   Pmts Frequency   Next Date   Account

Descri...

Register

Sched. Txns

Sort by: Next Date

My Accounts   Bills   Planning   Investments   Home & Car   Online   Reports

Now carry out the additional steps on page 113.

...cont'd

To continue setting up a transaction group, carry out the following steps:

3 Click here

REMEMBER

Complete the following fields:

• Frequency
• Register Entry
• Days in Advance
before **you carry out step 7.**

4 Enter an effective date for the 1st Register entry

5 Click here; select an account in the list

6 Name the group

7 Click here

Carry out the following additional steps:

9 Click here when you've selected enough transactions

Assign Transactions to Group: 2

Description	Amount	Type	Memo	Cat	Clr	Grp
Beefeater	-59.95	Pmt		Dining		
Boots	-10.00	Pmt		Medical		
British Gas	-128.89	Chq		Utilities:Gas		
British Teleco...	-23.47	%Spl	Split for J...	Utilities:H...		
Byte Computer...	-25.00	Pmt	Printer Ca...	Purchases		
Cash Withdra...	-20.00	Pmt				
Contribution to...	-1,000.00	Pmt		[Mark P's...		
Hotel de France	-179.64	Pmt	F1,500.00	Taxes		
Janes Wages	351.50	Spl		Employm...		
Jody's salary	775.00	Spl	Jody's sal...	Employm...		
Jody's salary	775.00	Spl	Jody's sal...	Employm...		
Joe's Wages	698.00	Spl		Employm...		
Marks & Spen...	-25.00	Pmt		Home Re...		

☐ View Locked Items Only

REMEMBER

Re step 8 – repeat this for as many transactions as you want to include in the group. Then carry out step 9.

8 Double-click a transaction to include it in the group

The result:

Scheduled Transaction List / Standing Order List

New... Edit... Delete   Pay   Close

Description	Amount	Pmts	Frequency	Next Date	Account
British Gas	-43.68		Monthly	26/03/98 (Thursd...	Current
[Group 2] Entertainm...			Monthly	27/03/98 (Fri...	Current

Sort by: Next Date ▾

The new transaction group

Using transaction groups

To make Quicken enter a transaction group into the relevant account, pull down the Lists menu and click Scheduled Transaction. Now do the following:

HANDY TIP

Groups (to distinguish them from other scheduled transactions) are prefaced with 'Group' followed by a numeral and name (see the excerpt below):

2 Click here

Group name

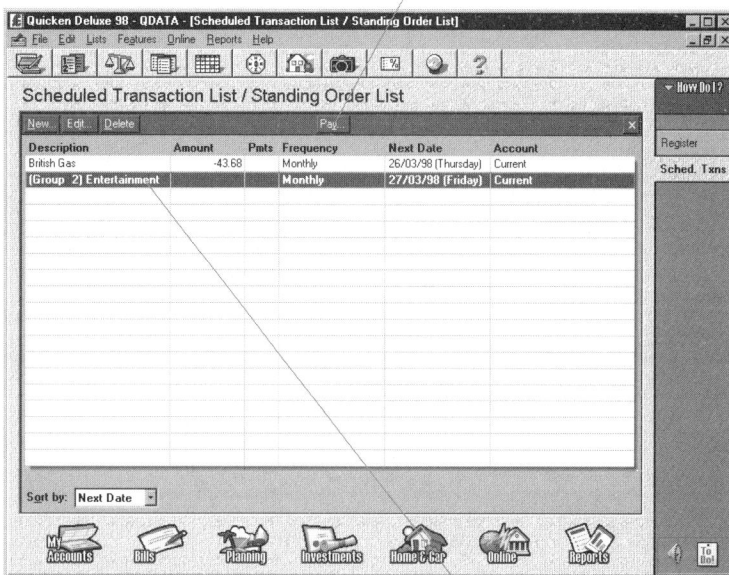

Highlight a transaction group

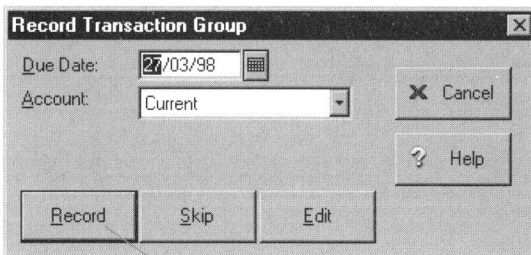

3 Click here to insert the group

Amending transaction group details

It's sometimes necessary to revise the details of transaction groups you've already set up.

You can:

- modify which account the group relates to

- include new transactions or exclude pre-assigned transactions

- modify the group name

- modify the payment frequency

- modify whether or not confirmation is required before entry

- modify the number of payments

- modify the extent of the postdating (if any)

Revising group details

Pull down the Lists menu and do the following:

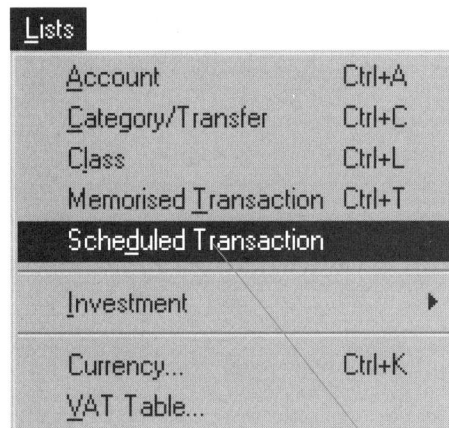

Lists	
Account	Ctrl+A
Category/Transfer	Ctrl+C
Class	Ctrl+L
Memorised Transaction	Ctrl+T
Scheduled Transaction	
Investment	▶
Currency...	Ctrl+K
VAT Table...	

Click here

...cont'd

HANDY TIP **Carry out steps 2 and 3. Then follow step 4 to amend the appropriate group details. Carry out step 5.**

To add new transactions (or remove existing ones) follow steps 6-7 as often as necessary

Finally, carry out step 8.

To continue revising group details, do the following (and see the tip):

3 Click here

2 Highlight a transaction group

5 Click here

4 Make any necessary alterations

7 Click here

8 Click here

6 Click a transaction

Deleting transaction groups

To delete a transaction group you've already set up, pull down the Lists menu and do the following:

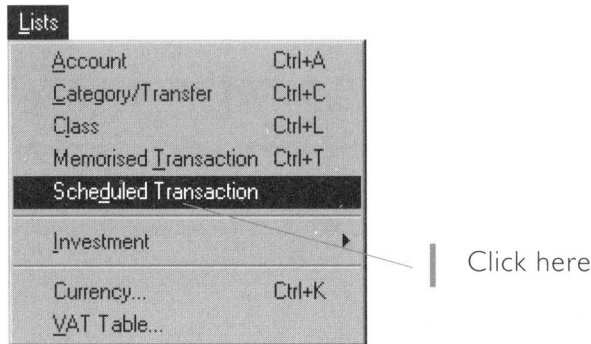

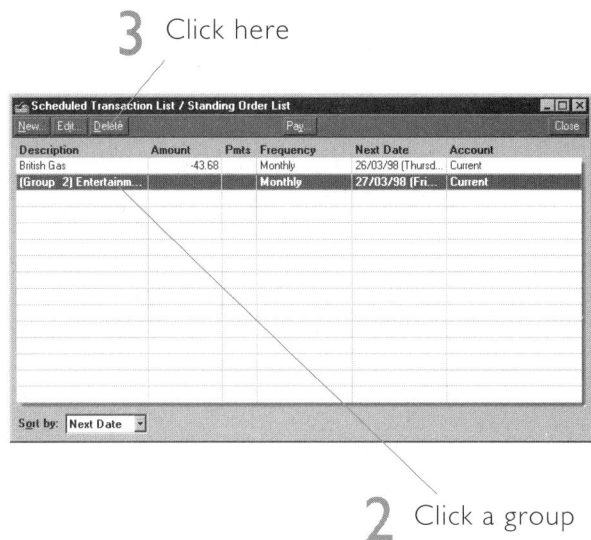

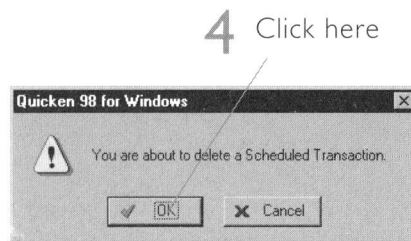

Click here

Click here

Click a group

Click here

Cheques

Use this chapter to learn how to have Quicken print your cheques for you. First, you'll enter cheques (as transactions) into a special dialog. Then you'll discover how to locate specific cheques, and – if necessary – how to delete or void them. In the next stage, you'll get Quicken ready to print them. Finally, you'll print out pending cheques and correct any alignment errors.

Covers

Chapter Six

Cheques – an overview

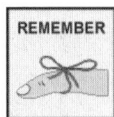

REMEMBER

The only part of the production process which Quicken can't automate is cheque signing.

When you've set up your Quicken account(s), you can go on handwriting cheques if you want, simply entering them into the Register as transactions as and when necessary. However, there is an alternative: you can have Quicken automate the entire process.

There are advantages to having Quicken print cheques:

- you save the time and effort of handwriting them

- details are entered into the Register automatically, thereby obviating the risk of error

- cheques look better – and more professional – when they're printed out

BEWARE

Note, however, that once a cheque *has* been printed out, no further amendments can be made.

- the cheque-writing process allows plenty of scope for you to change your mind before initiating printing. Unprinted cheques can be edited in situ, within the Register, or in a special dialog

However, there is also one proviso: you can only print cheques onto special stationery which can be ordered direct from Intuit MarketPlace (see the documentation which came with Quicken for more information on how to do this).

Categorising cheques

You can make the cheque-writing process very precise by:

— applying categories/sub-categories to cheque transactions

— applying classes/sub-classes to cheque transactions

— splitting cheque transactions

An example of a split cheque would be a multiple payment to an insurance company. If you're paying more than one premium at a time (because they fall due more or less simultaneously), you can ensure the transaction shows the split between the relevant departments.

Writing a cheque

Automating cheque production in Quicken is a two-stage process:

1. writing the cheque

2. printing it out

Writing a cheque

First, press Ctrl+A. Do the following:

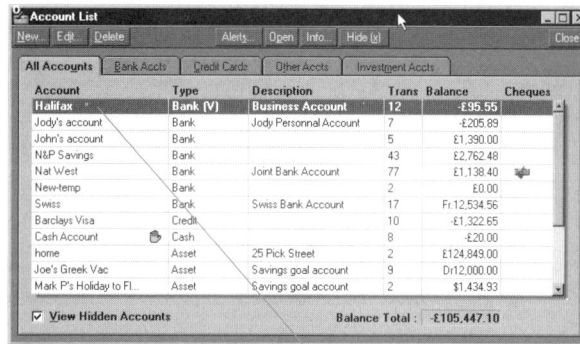

Double-click the account into which you want the cheque inserted

Quicken opens the account. Now pull down the Features menu and do the following:

2 Click here

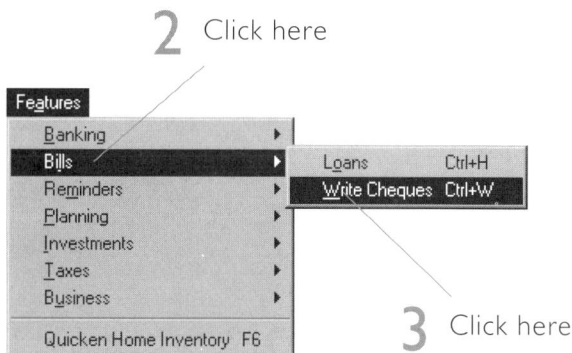

3 Click here

REMEMBER

Type in address details in the Address field, only if you're sending the cheque out in a *window* envelope.

REMEMBER

By default, Quicken inserts the current date in the Date field.

If this isn't what you want, type in the correct date.

BEWARE

Re step 6 – any text you type in the Memo field may be visible if you send the cheque out in a window envelope.

HANDY TIP

To split a cheque, follow the procedures on page 123, *before* you carry out step 9.

Now carry out steps 4-5 below. Follow step 6 if you want to insert a short description and/or steps 7-8 to apply a category to the cheque (to apply a class instead, type it in in the normal way in step 7 and ignore step 8). Finally, follow step 9 (but see the HANDY TIP first if you need to 'split' the cheque).

5 Type in payee details   4 Type in the amount

Write Cheques: Halifax (£)

Delete | Find   Print... | Options... | Report ▼ | Close

Pay to the Order of The Five Bells   Date 28/03/98

£ 74.24

Seventy-Four Pounds and 24 Pence***

Address   High Street
          Penge

Memo

9 Click here

Category Entertainment   Split...   Record Cheque

Cheques to Print

Date	Type	Payee	Category	Amount
28/03/98				

Ending Balance: -95.55

Nat West | N&P Savings | Swiss | Halifax | Jody's account | John's acc >

6 Optional – type in brief descriptive text

7 Click here

Commission	Expense
Covenants	Expense
Dining	Expense
Drawings	Expense
Education	Expense
Entertain	Expense
Entertainment	**Expense**
Gardening	Expense

Split...

8 Click a category

Splitting the cheque

If you need to 'split' a cheque, follow steps 4-8 (as appropriate) on page 122. Then click this button in the Write Cheques dialog:

Split...

Now carry out the additional steps below:

A Apply or create the relevant category or class

B Type in the amount for the split component

REMEMBER

Quicken updates the balance here as you enter the split:

Split Transaction Window

Use this window to itemise the transaction, and get more detail.

	Category	VAT	Memo	Amount	VAT Amount
1.	Entertainment			64 24	0 00
2.	Tip			10 00	0 00
3.			Next Edit ▾		
4.					
5.					
6.					
7.					

	Split Total:	74.24
	Remainder:	0.00
Adjust...	Transaction Total:	74.24

✓ OK   ✗ Cancel   ? Help

Hint: if there is some amount leftover, use the adjust button to get rid of it ->

C Click here

Repeat steps A and B for as many components as you want to include in the split. Carry out step C when you've finished creating it.

Finally, to complete creation of the cheque, follow step 9 on page 122.

Cheque searches

Another advantage to having Quicken both prepare and print your cheques is that you can write multiple cheques in one or more sittings and store them up until it's convenient to print them. Unprinted cheques are stored in the Write Cheques dialog and classed as *pending*.

Because unprinted cheques can rapidly accumulate, Quicken helps you find the one you want by allowing you to search for numbers and/or text with just a few mouse clicks.

For example, if you know a cheque has a specific amount or payee, you can search for this. Or if you're not sure of the precise details, you can use wildcards (or 'match characters').

Wildcards

You can use Quicken's standard 'match characters' in cheque searches:

?   stands for any single character

..   stands for any number of (unspecified) characters

~   tells Quicken to ignore matches for any following text

Search criteria

You can make cheque searches more precise by restricting them to:

- a specific field

- a specific type of match

For full details of match types, see page 81.

Running a cheque search

To locate a specific pending cheque, pull down the Features menu and do the following:

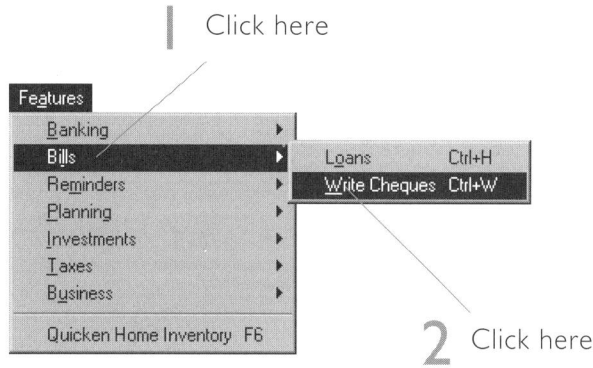

1 Click here

Features
  Banking   ▶
  Bills   ▶   Loans   Ctrl+H
  Reminders   ▶   Write Cheques Ctrl+W
  Planning   ▶
  Investments   ▶
  Taxes   ▶
  Business   ▶

  Quicken Home Inventory F6   2 Click here

4 Click here

REMEMBER

Pending cheques are displayed in this section of the Write Cheques dialog:

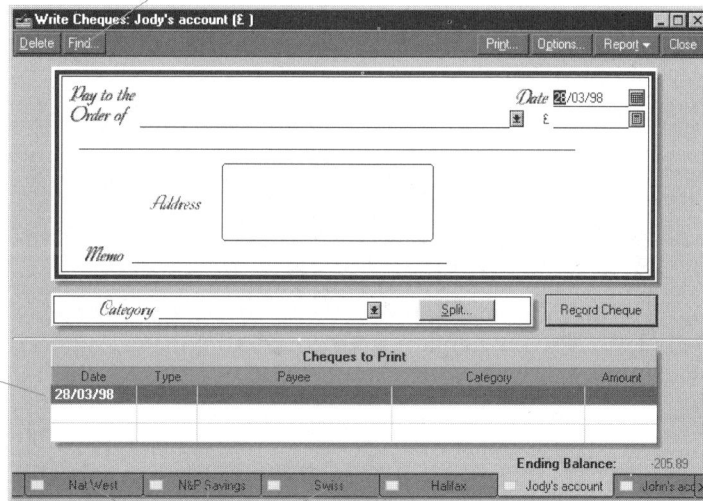

Write Cheques: Jody's account (£)

Delete Find...   Print... Options... Report ▾ Close

Pay to the
Order of   Date 28/03/98
                                            ▲ £

          Address

          Memo

Category   ▲   Split...   Record Cheque

Cheques to Print

Date	Type	Payee	Category	Amount
28/03/98				

                                          Ending Balance: -205.89

  Nat West   N&P Savings   Swiss   Halifax   Jody's account   John's acc >

3 Click the button which relates to the relevant account

Follow the additional steps on page 126.

Now carry out step 5 below. To restrict the search, follow steps 6-7 and/or 8-9, as appropriate. Finally, carry out step 10 to have Quicken locate the first matching cheque and display it within the Write Cheques dialog, OR step 11 to have it compile a list of matches (see page 127).

HANDY TIP

Click the Close button when you've finished searching for cheques.

5 Type in search data

10 Click here

Quicken Find

Find:	Magnet Restaurant	Find
Search:	All Fields ▾	Find All
Match if:	Contains ▾	Close
	☑ Search Backwards	Help

6 Click here   8 Click here   11 Click here

All Fields
Amount
Cleared Status
Memo
Date
Category/Class
Cheque Number
Payee

7 Optional – restrict the search to a specific field

Contains
Exact
Starts With
Ends With
Greater
Greater or Equal
Less
Less or Equal

9 Apply a match type

Multiple finds

If you carried out a search using step 11 on page 126, Quicken – instead of displaying the first cheque in the Write Cheques window – launches a special dialog listing *all* matching cheques (and other transactions).

Do the following to enter a cheque into the relevant account:

step 11 on page 126

HANDY TIP

In the Quicken Find dialog, unprinted cheques have 'Print' set against them:

Acct	Num
Jody's ac...	103
Nat West	Print
Nat West	Print
Nat West	Print

Denotes a cheque

Double-click a cheque entry

The Result:

The cheque entry within the Register

Deleting/voiding – an overview

Sometimes, cheques need to be deleted or voided. It's important to be clear about the distinction.

Deleting/voiding

Deletion permanently removes cheque details from the host account. Just about the only valid reason to delete a cheque entry is if you happen to have entered the wrong cheque number.

Voiding, on the other hand, is much more useful. Use it:

* when the cheque has been mislaid or lost

* when the cheque has been printed incorrectly

* to stop payment

When a cheque has been voided, Quicken inserts the following:

VOID

against its entry in the Write Cheque dialog.

A voided cheque

Deleting cheques

To delete a cheque, pull down the Features menu and do the following:

Click here

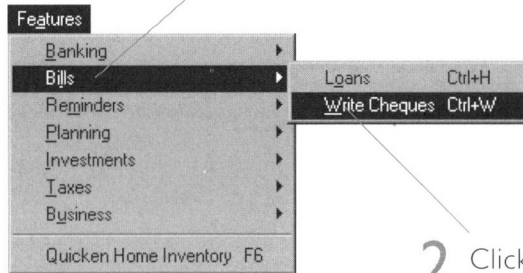

You can use a keyboard shortcut instead of carrying out step 5.
Simply press Ctrl+D.

2 Click here

5 Click here

After step 5, Quicken launches a warning message. Do the following:

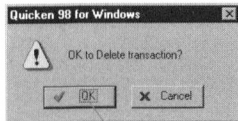

Click here

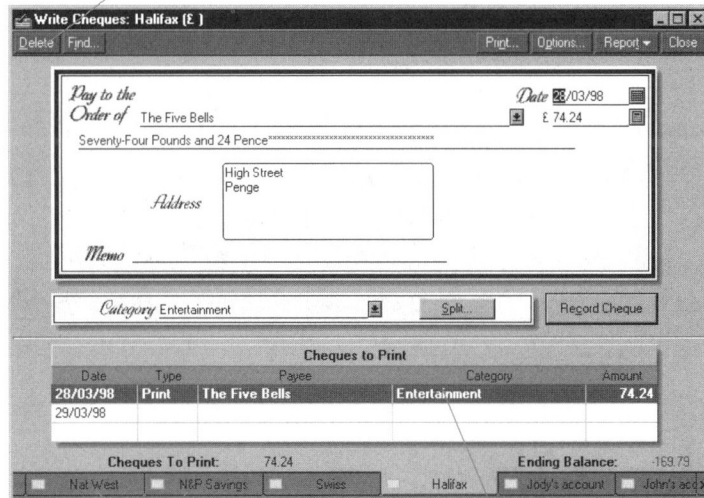

To close the Write Cheques window when you've finished with it, press Esc.

3 Select a host account

4 Select the cheque you want to delete

Voiding cheques

To void a cheque, pull down the Features menu and do the following:

You can only void a cheque if you've recorded it in the appropriate register.

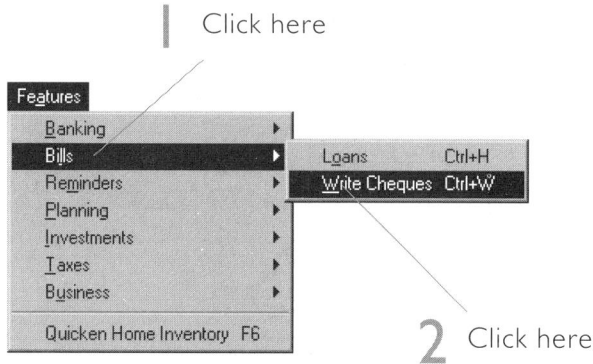

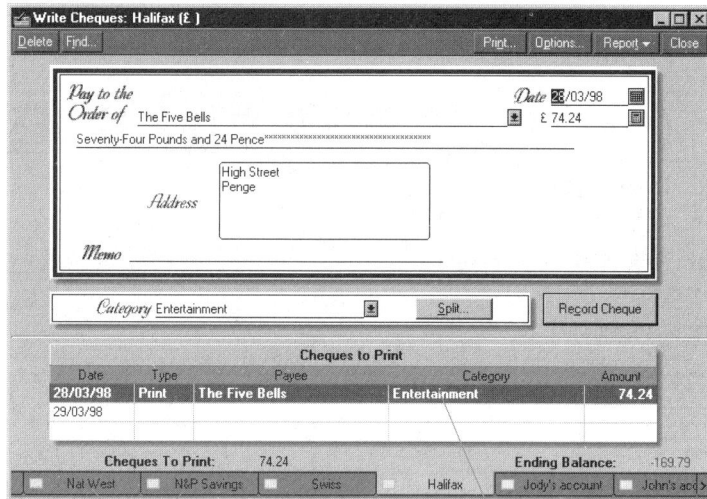

Click here

Features	
Banking	▶
Bills	▶
Reminders	▶
Planning	▶
Investments	▶
Taxes	▶
Business	▶
Quicken Home Inventory F6	

Loans	Ctrl+H
Write Cheques	Ctrl+W

2 Click here

Write Cheques: Halifax (£)

Delete Find...   Print... Options... Report ▾ Close

Pay to the
Order of The Five Bells   *Date* 28/03/98

Seventy-Four Pounds and 24 Pence**************************************   £ 74.24

Address   High Street
                 Penge

Memo

Category Entertainment   Split...   Record Cheque

Cheques to Print

Date	Type	Payee	Category	Amount
28/03/98	Print	The Five Bells	Entertainment	74.24
29/03/98				

Cheques To Print: 74.24   Ending Balance: -169.79

Nat West   N&P Savings   Swiss   Halifax   Jody's account   John's acc▶

To close the Write Cheques window when you've finished with it, press Esc.

3 Select a host account

4 Select the cheque you want to void

You can use a keyboard shortcut here. Simply press Ctrl+V.

Now pull down the Edit menu and click Transaction, Void Transaction. Finally, click this button:

Record Cheque

Getting ready to print cheques

If you elect to have Quicken print out your cheques, you should bear in mind the following:

- you have to use proprietary cheque forms supplied by Intuit MarketPlace

- these proprietary cheques are supplied in two formats:

  - Continuous

  - Page-Oriented

REMEMBER **This division isn't absolutely hard and fast. For instance, some dot matrix printers work with separate sheets of paper.**

Continuous cheques
These are suitable for printers which operate with tractor-feed mechanisms i.e. daisywheel and dot matrix printers.

Page-Oriented cheques
These are designed with paper-trays in mind, and are therefore suitable for laser and inkjet printers.

You have to tell Quicken which cheque format is correct before you begin printing.

The following additional factors also have to be taken into account. You need to ensure that:

— the correct printer is selected

— the correct cheque style is selected

— the correct font and type size have been allocated

— your printer's internal settings are correctly set

— (if you want to print incomplete pages of cheques) the correct layout is selected

— you carry out a sample print run to correct any misalignment problems *before* you print the final version of the cheque. (See page 136.)

Print setup

Pull down the File menu and carry out steps 1-2 below:

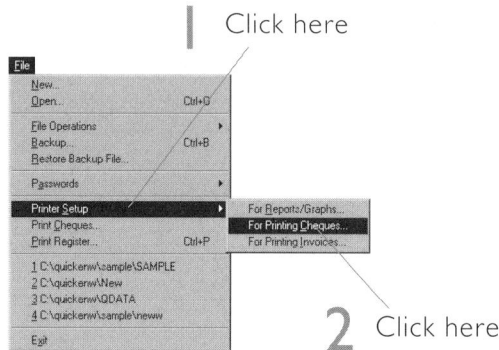

⎮ Click here

2 Click here

Now carry out step 3 (if you have more than one printer installed) and then step 4. Carry out step 5 to use nonstandard cheque types, and/or step 6 if you're printing incomplete pages of cheques. Follow step 7 to set your printer's internal settings (for how to complete the resultant dialog, see your printer's manual). Finally, carry out step 8.

For how to set cheque font and type size preferences, see page 133.

For how to correct alignment problems, see page 136.

Re step 6 – these settings determine the way the sheet is inserted into the printer.

3 Click here; select the correct printer from the list

4 Select a feed type

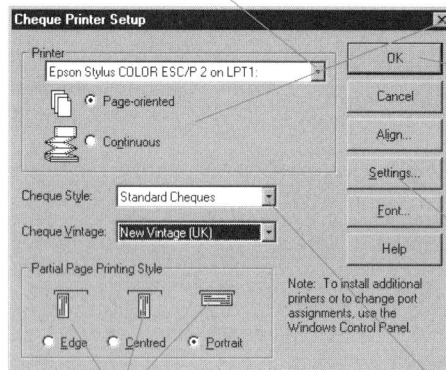

8 Click here

7 Click here

6 Choose a layout

5 Click here; select a style in the list

Setting font preferences

Pull down the File menu and click Printer Setup, For Printing Cheques. Now carry out the following steps, as appropriate:

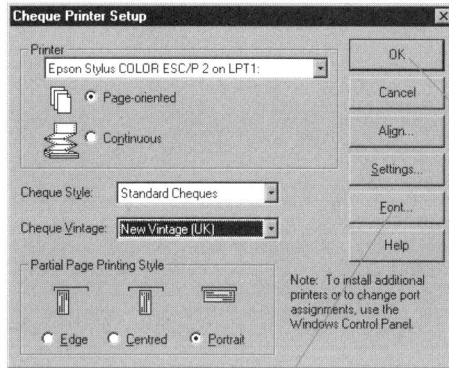

5 Click here

| Click here

2 Select a new typeface   3 Type in a new type size

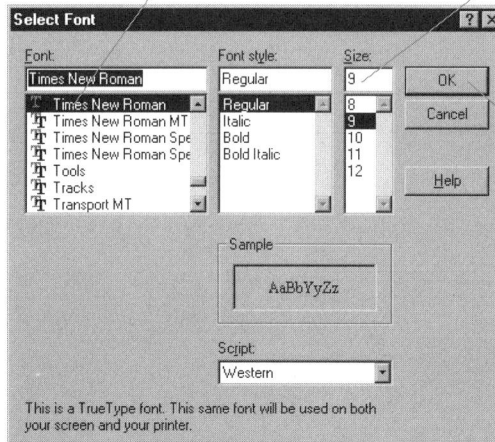

4 Click here

Printing cheques

Once you've implemented the correct printer settings (see pages 131-133), you can print out your cheques.

By default, Quicken assumes you want to print *all* cheques which are currently pending within the Write Cheques dialog. However, if you don't want to do this, you can instead:

Don't forget to sign your cheques when you've printed them.

- restrict the cheques printed to those which fall within a specific date range. You do this by specifying a date beyond which cheques will not be printed

- manually select cheques

You can also:

- customise the number of cheques printed per page

- print multiple cheque copies

- select a nonstandard cheque style

Before you start a print-run

Carry out the following actions before you begin to print your cheques:

A. ensure your printer has been switched on

B. ensure you've inserted the necessary cheque forms from Intuit MarketPlace

C. make a note of the number on the first cheque (you'll need to insert this later into the Select Cheques to Print dialog – see step 1 on page 135)

D. open the account which contains the cheques which require to be printed (or select it in the Account List dialog)

...cont'd

Starting a print-run

Follow steps A-D on page 134. Then pull down the File menu and click Print Cheques. Now carry out step 1 below. Follow step 2 if you want to apply a date restriction. Carry out step 3 to specify the sheet layout. Perform steps 4-6 if you want to select cheques manually. If you want to print multiple cheque copies, follow step 7. Finally, carry out step 8 to begin printing.

REMEMBER

Re step 1 – insert the number you noted in step C on page 134.

1 Insert the first cheque number

2 Click here, then type in an end date

8 Click here

HANDY TIP

If you need to use a non-standard cheque style, click the button to the right of the Cheque Style field. Select a style from the list. Then complete the rest of the dialog as appropriate. Finally, follow step 8.

3 Specify the no. of cheques per page

4 Click Selected Cheques, then the Options button

7 Specify the no. of copies

6 Click here

5 Select one or more cheques

Correcting misalignment

HANDY TIP

Quicken may display this button:

Print Sample

while you're correcting any misalignment. Click it to have Quicken print a sample cheque, complete with an alignment grid, on blank paper.
   Place the printout over a real cheque, then hold both up to the light; use the grid to gauge the extent of any necessary realignment.

If, when you come to print out your cheque(s), the text isn't correctly aligned within the cheque form, carry out the following procedure.

Pull down the File menu and click Printer Setup, Cheque Printer Setup. Now carry out step 1 below:

Cheque Printer Setup	
Printer	OK
Epson Stylus COLOR ESC/P 2 on LPT1:	Cancel
○ Page-oriented	Align...
○ Continuous	Settings...
Cheque Style: Standard Cheques	Font...
Cheque Vintage: New Vintage (UK)	Help
Partial Page Printing Style	Note: To install additional printers or to change port assignments, use the Windows Control Panel.
○ Edge ○ Centred ● Portrait	

2 Click here

Click here

The dialog which now launches depends on:

• the cheque style chosen in the Cheque Style field (see step 5 on page 132)

REMEMBER

Repeat the realignment process as often as necessary, until cheques print correctly.

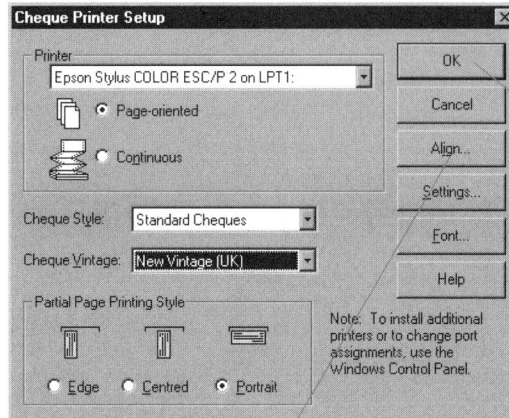

• whether Page-oriented or Continuous is chosen (see step 4 on page 132)

Simply follow the on-screen instructions.

Finally, when you've finished correcting the misalignment, carry out step 2 above.

Reconciliation

Use this chapter to learn how to 'reconcile' (harmonise) your accounts with your bank statements. You'll use various techniques to compare deposits and withdrawals against statement entries, and isolate any discrepancies. Once located, inconsistencies can be adjusted easily and conveniently, or – if small – written off. Finally, you'll confirm that reconciliation is complete and – optionally – print out a reconciliation report.

Covers

Chapter Seven

Reconciliation – an overview

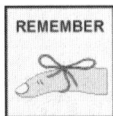

Because Current accounts have more variables than Bldg. Society accounts (e.g. there are bank charges to be taken into account), we'll concentrate on them in this chapter.

Quicken Current and Bldg. Society accounts have to be 'reconciled' against records kept by your bank or building society. In essence, reconciliation simply involves verifying that transactions in your account match those in your bank statement or passbook.

In rather more detail, reconciliation is the process of:

1. transposing bank statement information (for example, bank charges and interest payments) into the corresponding Quicken account

2. comparing the bank statement with the account and marking as 'cleared' those transactions which are identical in both

3. totalling the number of cleared items in both the statement and account, and making sure the two totals tally

4. resolving any instances where the statement and account *don't* tally (this is itself a two-part process)

**Some other account types also have to be reconciled e.g. Investment.
  With these accounts, the process is basically the same, though abbreviated. Simply follow the on-screen instructions, using the procedures in this chapter as a guide.**

It is, however, important to bear in mind that you won't necessarily perform all 4 steps (and the order may vary).

Initial reconciliation

Normally, reconciliation is straightforward enough. However, when you reconcile an account for the first time, the situation can become rather more complex. This is because the initial setting up of an account involves inserting, as the opening balance, the balance on your latest statement.

This is all well and good provided that there were no outstanding transactions (withdrawals or deposits which hadn't yet appeared on the statement) at the time. If reconciling the account demonstrates that there were, you have the following options:

The second method is most often required. (See pages 147-150 for more information).

•   adjusting the opening balance

•   allowing Quicken to make its own adjustment at the end of reconciliation

Reconciling an account – stage 1

Press Ctrl+A, then carry out the following steps:

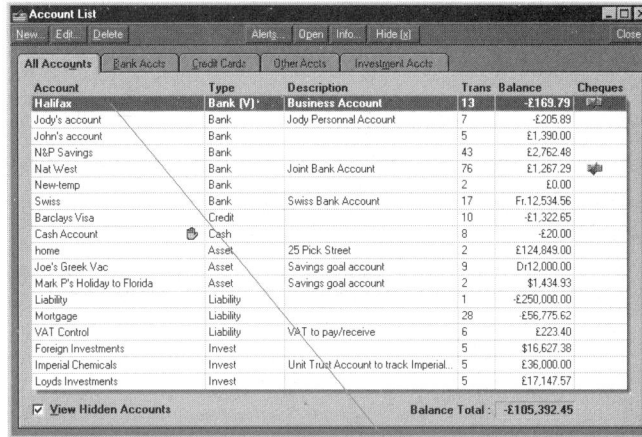

| Click the account you want to reconcile

Pull down the Features menu and do the following:

2 Click here

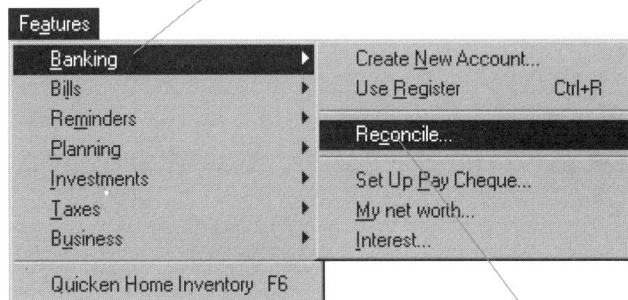

3 Click here

Now carry out steps 4-8 below. Follow step 9 if you want to allocate a revised category/sub-category or class/sub-class combination to the interest and charge entries. Finally, perform step 10:

REMEMBER

Step 4 only applies to accounts which are being reconciled for the first time.

4 If this figure *isn't* your statement's opening balance, delete it. Type in your opening balance

5 Insert the statement's final balance

Reconcile Bank Statement: Halifax

1. Enter the following from your bank statement.

Opening Balance: 5,008.00

Ending Balance:

2. Enter and categorise your interest and bank charges, if any.

Service Charge: Date: 01/02/97

Category: Bank Chrg

Interest Earned: Date: 30/10/97

Category: Int Inc

✓ OK   ✗ Cancel   ? Help

6 Insert the total service charges

7 Insert the correct charge dates

REMEMBER

Re step 9 – note that Quicken selects and applies the relevant Service Charge and interest Earned categories automatically; change these if necessary.

10 Click here

9 Optional – apply a new category or class

8 Insert total interest payments

In the next stage of the reconciliation process, Quicken lists all deposits and withdrawals in your account and invites you to compare them with your statement.

See page 141.

Reconciling an account – stage 2

In Bldg. Society accounts (here and subsequently), for 'statement' read 'passbook'.

After step 10 on page 140, Quicken launches a special dialog. You use this to compare entries on your statement with those in the relevant Quicken account – all transactions are listed, in date order. This is a crucial component of the reconciliation process. Fortunately, Quicken makes it easy and convenient.

Even more helpfully, in the normal course of events the entries will correspond exactly – the ideal situation. When this is the case, you tell Quicken as much and each ratified transaction is marked with:

in the Clr ('Cleared') field. Each time you ratify a transaction, Quicken adjusts the running totals in the bottom right-hand corner of the dialog.

The illustration below provides definitions of the three totals:

The opening account balance – as you ratify entries, Quicken adjusts this figure

Cleared Balance:	5,000.00
Statement Ending Balance:	-169.79
Difference:	**5,169.79**

This field is updated as reconciliation proceeds. Reconciliation is complete when it shows: **0.00**

The final statement balance

For what to do if the Difference field *doesn't* register 0.00 after reconciliation, see page 143.

...cont'd

REMEMBER

If the Difference field *doesn't* show 0.00 **at this stage, see the Note: section at the bottom of this page.**

Now carry out step 1 below. Repeat for all transactions shown. Follow step 2 if, at the end of this stage, the Difference field (at the base of the dialog) shows 0.00.

Click any entry which has an exact equivalent in your statement

HANDY TIP

These entries: are used in stage 3 of the reconciliation process – see page 143.

2 Click here

Note:

If, when all transactions have been ratified in step 1, the Difference field doesn't show 0.00, *don't* carry out step 2 above.

Instead, refer to page 143.

Reconciling an account – stage 3

In this stage of the reconciliation process, we assume that – at the end of stage 2 on page 142 – the Difference field didn't register 0.00. That it didn't means there is a discrepancy.

There are several measures you can take to correct discrepancies between your account and statement. The first is the simplest, and often the most effective. Count the number of deposits in your statement, then compare this with the following field:

0 deposits, credits

Compare this number with the total
number of deposits in your account

in the Reconcile Bank Statement dialog (see page 142).

Now compare the total number of withdrawals with the following:

1 cheque, debit

Compare this number with the total
number of withdrawals in your account

in the Reconcile Bank Statement dialog (see page 142).

You should also total deposit and withdrawal amounts on your statement. Compare these with the totals shown to the right of the fields mentioned above.

When you've isolated where the account/statement discrepancies lie, move on to stage 4 on page 144.

Reconciling an account – stage 4

The techniques on page 143 will have isolated where the discrepancy between your account and statement lies. The next – and final – stage is to resolve it. There are two basic possibilities:

A. The fault lies with your bank, in that they have entered one or more transactions wrongly. All you can do in this situation is contact the bank and get it to correct the error. In the interim, don't mark the relevant transaction as cleared

B. *You* have entered one or more transactions wrongly. Or you haven't entered one or more transactions which appear on the statement and which are correct (for example, a salary deposit). In either case, you can easily rectify the problem yourself

REMEMBER

For how to resolve situation B by inserting one or more omitted transactions, see page 146.

Resolving situation B. by amending a transaction

These actions follow on directly from steps 1-2 on page 142.

With the Reconcile Bank Statement dialog open, do the following:

4 Click here

HANDY TIP

Re step 3 – ensure the relevant Clr field does not contain:

3 Click a transaction which needs to be revised in your account

...cont'd

Now do the following:

6 Click here

7 Click here

HANDY TIP

When a Register entry has been cleared, Quicken inserts 'R' in the Clr field:

5 Revise the transaction appropriately

Payment	Clr
Exp	
	R

In the Reconcile Bank Account dialog, do the following:

REMEMBER

Re step 8 – if the Difference field doesn't show 0.00, **follow the procedures on page 147.**

8 If the Difference field shows 0.00, click the Finished button.

...cont'd

REMEMBER

This procedure resolves problems where valid transactions have been omitted from your account.

For how to rectify reconciliation difficulties where transactions you *have* entered are wrong, see pages 144-145.

HANDY TIP

Don't forget to enter any direct debit amounts into the Register now (they weren't inserted when you set up the direct debits, because the amounts fluctuate).

REMEMBER

Re step 6 – if the Difference field doesn't show 0.00, follow the procedures on page 147.

Resolving situation ß by inserting a transaction

These actions follow on directly from steps 1-2 on page 142.

With the Reconcile Bank Statement dialog open, press Ctrl+R. Now do the following:

4 Click here

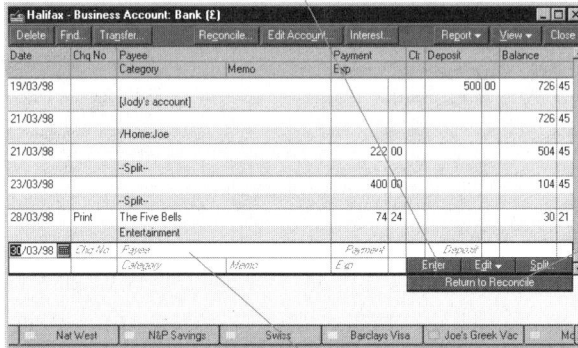

5 Click here

3 Insert the new transaction

In the Reconcile Bank Account dialog, do the following:

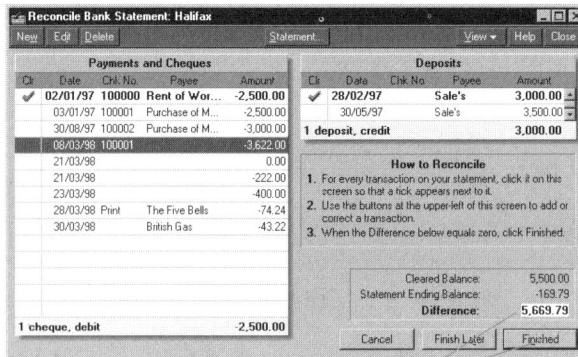

6 If the Difference field shows 0.00, click the Finished button.

If the figures still don't tally

If, after you've followed the procedures on pages 144-145 or 146, the Difference field in the Reconcile Bank Statement dialog still doesn't show 0.00, you can do either of the following:

A.   click the Finished button regardless (this writes off the inconsistency)

or

B.   carry on searching for the discrepancy until you locate it (if it's large, this should be possible)

Clearly, step A. is more applicable if the extent of the discrepancy is slight: writing off small amounts is much more acceptable. When you follow step A., Quicken inserts the appropriate adjustment into your account.

Follow step B. for larger discrepancies, but when you do bear in mind the following:

First time reconciliations

There is a special case which you need to be aware of. If BOTH of the following are true:

•   the discrepancy has arisen in an account which is being reconciled for the first time

•   the account was set up when there were outstanding transactions which hadn't yet cleared (see also pages 138 and 140)

the outstanding amount in the Difference field probably relates to the missing transactions. In this scenario, you'll want Quicken to adjust the account's Opening Balance accordingly.

Both approaches – writing off a small discrepancy and adjusting the Opening Balance to take into account missed transactions – are discussed in the next two pages.

Writing off a minor discrepancy

Within the Reconcile Bank Statement dialog, do the following:

REMEMBER

The discrepancy here is so small it can safely be written off:

Click here

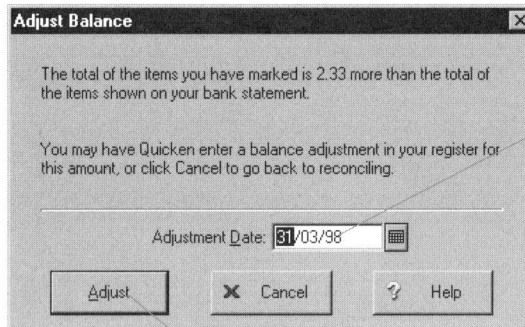

2 Type in a date

3 Click here to have Quicken make the relevant internal adjustment

...cont'd

Adjusting the Opening Balance

REMEMBER

The discrepancy here is larger and (in this case) relates to one or more transactions omitted at inception of the account:

Within the Reconcile Bank Statement dialog, do the following:

Reconcile Bank Statement: Current 2

New | Edit | Delete | Statement... | View ▾ | Help | Close

Payments and Cheques

Clr	Date	Chk No.	Payee	Amount
✔	05/01/98		J. Smith	-142.63
✔	08/01/98		British ...	-35.23

Deposits

Clr	Date	Chk No.	Payee	Amount

0 deposits, credits

272.14
5.00

Cleared
Statement Ending

267.14

2 cheques, debits   -177.86

Cancel

Finished

Click here

BEWARE

For this procedure to be applicable, you must have followed step 4 on page 140.

Adjust Balance

The total of the items you have marked is 267.14 more than the total of the items shown on your bank statement.

You may have Quicken enter a balance adjustment in your register for this amount, or click Cancel to go back to reconciling.

Adjustment Date: 31/03/98

Adjust   ✗ Cancel   ❓ Help

2 Type in a date

3 Click here to have Quicken make the relevant internal adjustment

The final hurdle

At this juncture, you've clicked the Finished button in the Reconcile Bank Statement dialog to signal that the reconciliation process is finished. Quicken now launches a special message. Do ONE of the following:

REMEMBER **This is the message which appears if reconciliation was successful, without the need to create an internal adjustment of any kind.**

If an adjustment *was* made, a different message appears. However, steps 1 and 2 (and 3-5, if appropriate) still apply.

Reconciliation Complete

Congratulations!

Your account is balanced. The items you have marked have been reconciled in your register.

Would you like to create a reconciliation report?

[✓ Yes] [⊘ No] [? Help]

2 Click here to return to the Register

| Click here to have Quicken print a reconciliation report

REMEMBER **For more information on reports, see Chapter 8.**

If you followed step 1, carry out the following:

3 Name the report

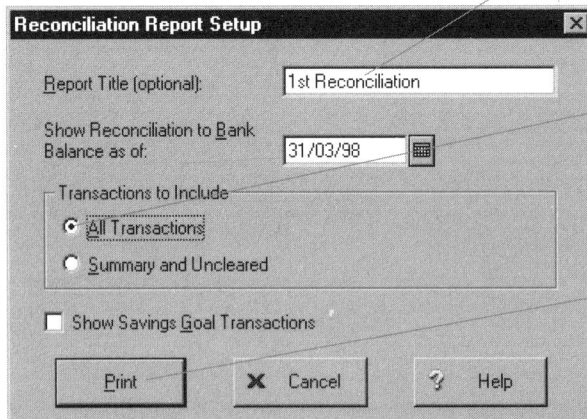

Reconciliation Report Setup

Report Title (optional):   1st Reconciliation

Show Reconciliation to Bank Balance as of: 31/03/98

Transactions to Include
  ● All Transactions
  ○ Summary and Uncleared

☐ Show Savings Goal Transactions

[Print] [✗ Cancel] [? Help]

4 Ensure this is selected

REMEMBER **Don't forget to make sure your printer is switched on and ready to print *before* you carry out steps 3-5.**

5 Click here

Reports and Graphs

Use this chapter to view your financial data as reports and graphs. You'll create standardised reports/graphs, and then learn how to specify which components display. You'll also memorise reports and graphs, for later recall. Finally, you'll print your report/graph.

Covers

Chapter Eight

Reports and graphs – an overview

Quicken makes managing your day-to-day finances easy. However, it's also vital to be able to take an overview of them. You can do this in two ways:

- textually, by generating reports

- visually, by generating graphs

Use Quicken's report formats to achieve a detailed written evaluation of your finances, based on the heading you select. Utilise its graphing capability to make a similar kind of evaluation *instantly*. Better still, use both reports and graphs for a comprehensive picture of how your finances are progressing.

REMEMBER

This is the report Customise bar:

Use it to:

- apply a preset date range to an existing report (by clicking the flagged field and choosing one in the drop-down list)
- apply a user-defined date range to an existing report (by typing in start and end dates in the From: and To: fields)

When you've done one of the above, click this button:

| Update |

to implement your changes.

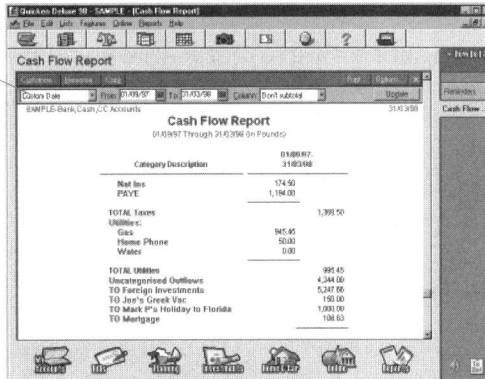

A sample report

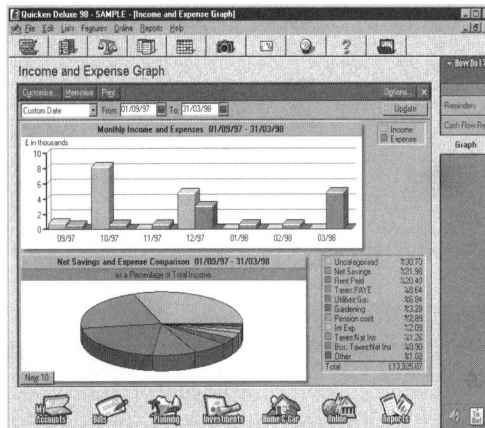

A sample graph

Report settings

Before you tell Quicken to generate a report, it's important to make sure report preferences are correctly set.

You can select:

- the date ranges used in selected report types (in effect, this is a filter: all transactions outside the specified range are excluded)

- whether accounts display names and/or descriptions

- whether categories display names and/or descriptions

- whether Quicken uses colours to denote negative amounts and headings

Setting report preferences

Pull down the Edit menu and do the following:

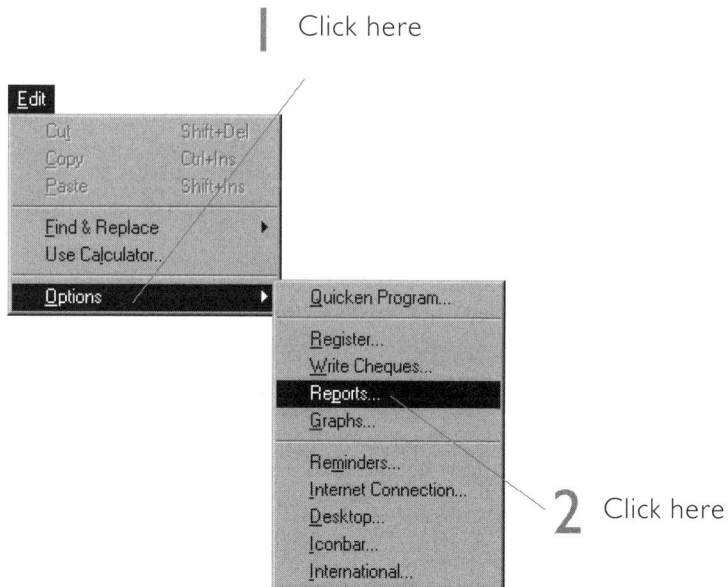

Click here

Edit

Cut	Shift+Del
Copy	Ctrl+Ins
Paste	Shift+Ins

Find & Replace   ▶
Use Calculator...

Options   ▶

Quicken Program...

Register...
Write Cheques...
Reports...
Graphs...

Reminders...
Internet Connection...
Desktop...
Iconbar...
International...

2 Click here

Now follow the additional steps on page 154.

Now do the following, as appropriate:

- carry out step 3 to set account display preferences

- carry out step 4 to set category display preferences

- carry out step 5 to impose a date range

- carry out step 6 to deselect colour in reports

- finally, carry out step 7 in all cases:

3 Click an option   4 Click an option   7 Click here

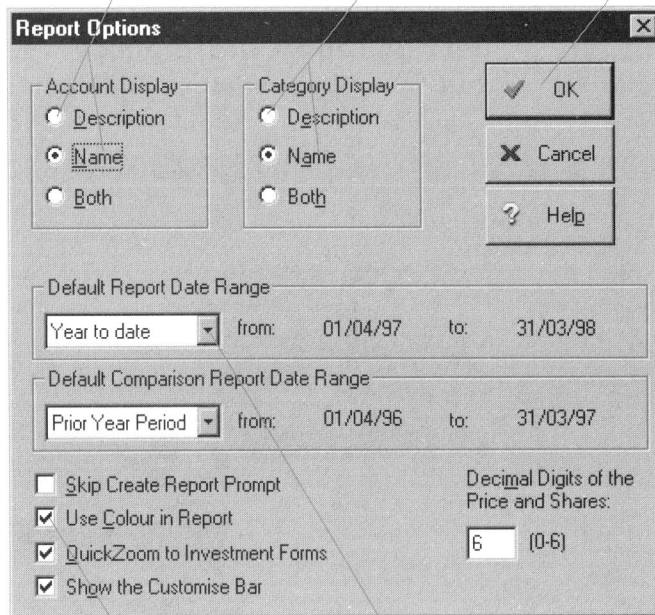

Report Options

Account Display
- ○ Description
- ● Name
- ○ Both

Category Display
- ○ Description
- ● Name
- ○ Both

✓ OK

✗ Cancel

? Help

Default Report Date Range

Year to date   from: 01/04/97   to: 31/03/98

Default Comparison Report Date Range

Prior Year Period   from: 01/04/96   to: 31/03/97

- ☐ Skip Create Report Prompt
- ☑ Use Colour in Report
- ☑ QuickZoom to Investment Forms
- ☑ Show the Customise Bar

Decimal Digits of the Price and Shares:

6   (0-6)

6 Click here   5 Click here; select a default date range in the drop-down list

Report types

Quicken offers three principal report types:

- Home

- Business

- Other

These are in turn divided into sub-types.

Home reports

Home report types include:

Itemised Categories	a list of transactions compiled in category order
Missing Cheques	locates omitted and duplicated cheques
Comparison	compares income/expense over a given period
Cash Flow	summarises income/expense by category
Net Worth	calculates your net worth based on the account balance

Business reports

Available Business reports include:

P&L Statement	compiles a profit and loss summary by category
A/P by Vendor	summarises outstanding bills under creditor sub-headings
A/P by Customer	summarises outstanding payments under customer sub-headings
Job/Project	summarises income/expense by classes

Other reports
These include:

Account Balances   summarises balances for your accounts

Summary   summarises transactions by categories (or any other item you specify)

Transaction   compiles transaction lists from one or more accounts

EasyAnswer reports
Quicken offers one more report type: EasyAnswer reports. EasyAnswer reports are based around a flexible question which you can customise at will.

Available EasyAnswer report types include:

*   Where did I spend my money…

*   How much did I spend on…

*   How much did I save…

*   What was I worth as of…

In some cases, you can also generate EasyAnswer graphs – see page 172.

Each report type is associated with one or more fields which you can use to fine-tune your report.

For example, the How much did I spend on…? EasyAnswer report provides the following variables:

> How much did I spend on ...?

Details:
Show spending on   Alimony paid
For the period   Year to date

Variable fields which make the report highly specific

Creating a standard report

The basis for report creation is the Create Report dialog.

To have Quicken compile a report for you, refer to the overhead Iconbar and carry out step 1 below:

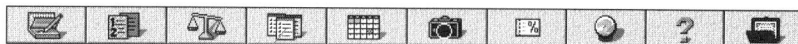

| Click here

Alternatively, pull down the Reports menu and carry out the following steps:

2 Click a report type

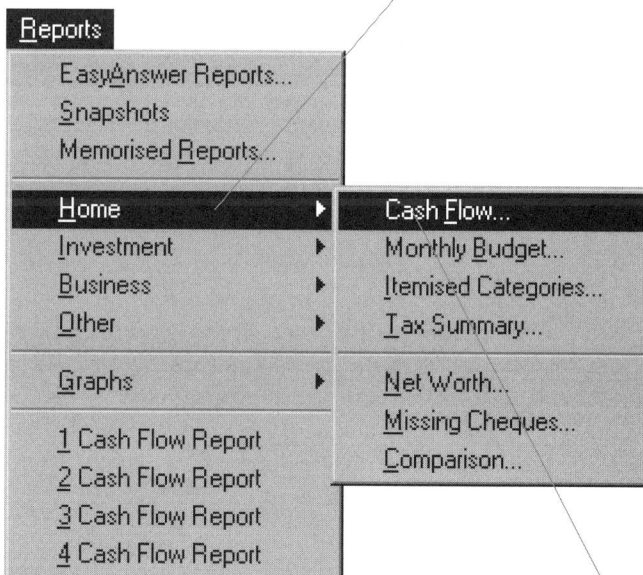

3 Click a sub-type

Now carry out the additional steps on page 158.

...cont'd

Carry out steps 4 and 5 below (but see the tip on the left). Carry out step 6 if you want to impose a preset date range, or 7 to apply your own date filter. Finally, perform step 8 to generate the chosen report:

REMEMBER

If you used the Reports menu to produce the Create Report dialog (steps 2-3 on page 157), it launches with the chosen sub-type already selected. You should therefore ignore steps 4 and 5.

4 Click a tab

7 Type in start and end dates

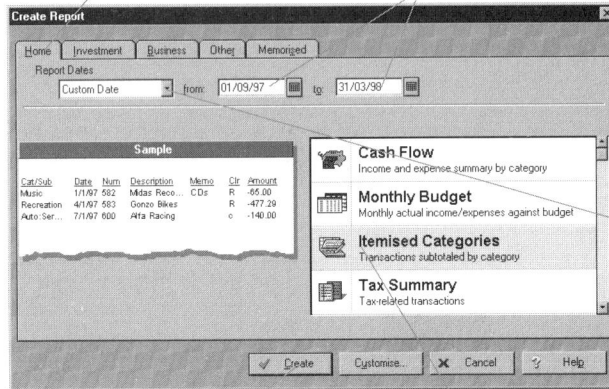

6 Click here; choose a range

8 Click here

5 Click a sub-type

The result – a Home/Itemised Categories report:

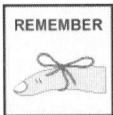

REMEMBER

This report was produced with an applied date range, in this case:
1st September 1997
to
31st March 1998

Creating an EasyAnswer report

Pull down the Reports menu and carry out the following steps:

Reports

- EasyAnswer Reports...
- Snapshots
- Memorised Reports...
- Home ▶
- Investment ▶
- Business ▶
- Other ▶
- Graphs ▶
- 1 Cash Flow Report
- 2 Itemised Categories Report
- 3 Itemised Categories Report
- 4 Cash Flow Report

1 Click here

HANDY TIP

You can use QuickZoom in reports. Move the mouse pointer over a report component (it changes to a magnifying glass). Double-click; Quicken launches a further report providing more detail on the original component.

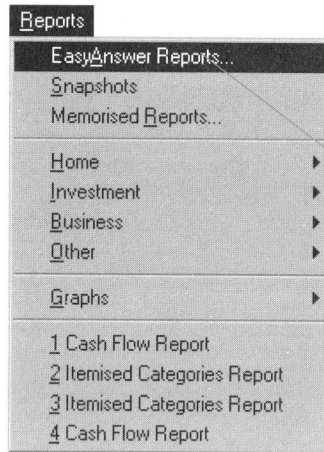

2 Click a question

3 Complete any subsidiary fields

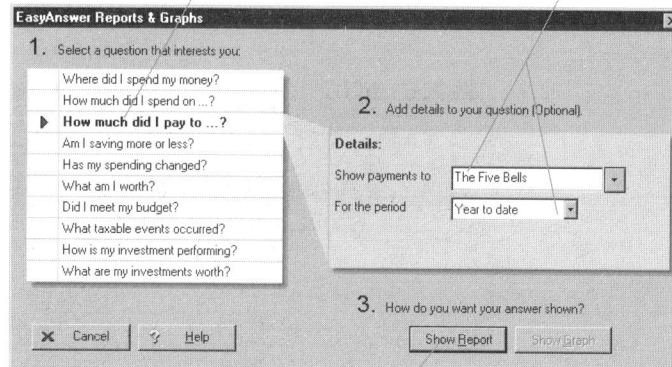

EasyAnswer Reports & Graphs

1. Select a question that interests you:
   - Where did I spend my money?
   - How much did I spend on ...?
   - **How much did I pay to ...?**
   - Am I saving more or less?
   - Has my spending changed?
   - What am I worth?
   - Did I meet my budget?
   - What taxable events occurred?
   - How is my investment performing?
   - What are my investments worth?

2. Add details to your question (Optional).

   Details:
   - Show payments to: The Five Bells
   - For the period: Year to date

3. How do you want your answer shown?

   Show Report   Show Graph

   ✗ Cancel   Help

4 Click here

Some sample EasyAnswer reports are shown on page 160.

The next illustration shows the resulting report:

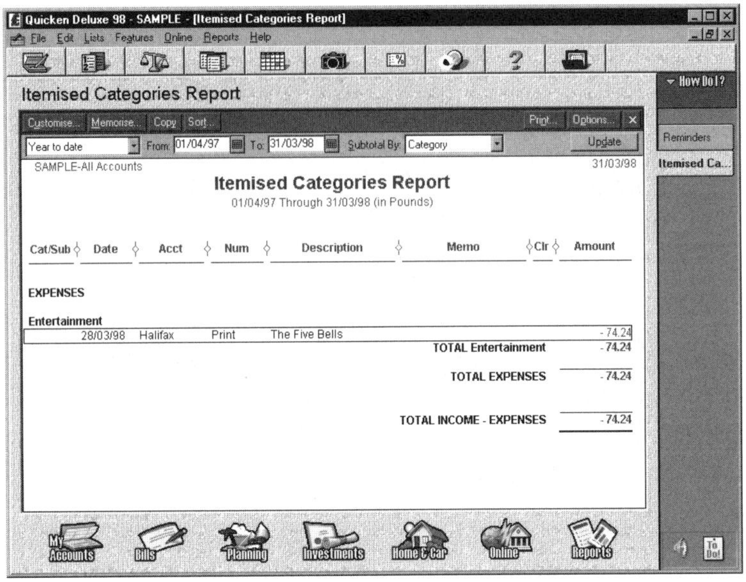

And another sample EasyAnswer report, this time a What am I worth? report time-limited to the current quarter:

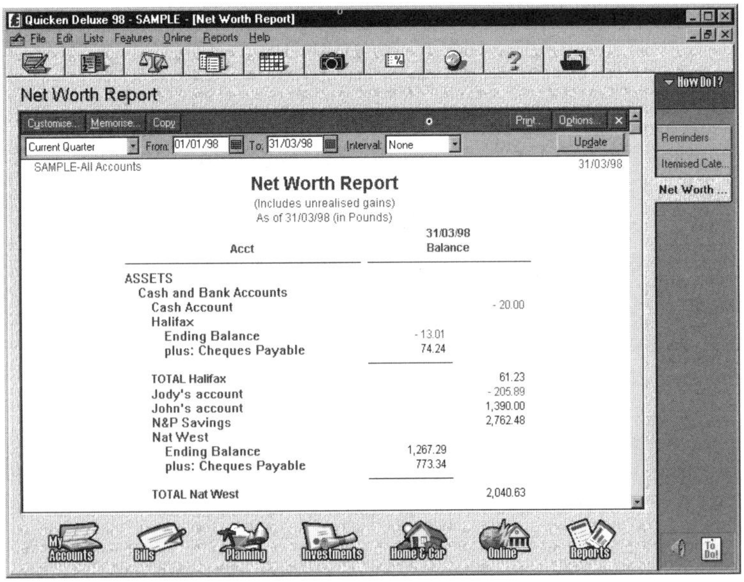

Customising reports

The procedures on pages 157-159 produce standardised reports. These are adequate for most purposes. However, when you become more experienced with Quicken you'll probably want to exercise more control.

You can:

To restrict the report to a specific transaction type (option D on the right), refer to page 162.

A. customise the report title, row and column headings and dates

B. include/exclude specific accounts

C. specify which transactions are included (on the basis of associated category or class)

D. limit the report to specific transaction types (for example, Deposits, Payments or Unprinted Cheques)

In step 6, however, click the Advanced tab. Now do the following:

Transaction Types: `Payments`

Click here; select a transaction type in the drop-down list

Finally, follow step 9 on page 162.

Quicken carries out these operations from within a special dialog.

The operations specified above are carried out from within the following dialog tabs:

A. the Display tab

B. the Accounts tab

C. the Include tab

D. the Advanced tab

Customising your report

Do the following to launch the Create Report dialog:

Click here

Now carry out the additional procedures on page 162.

...cont'd

REMEMBER

Re step 6 – this topic focuses on excluding specific accounts. If you need to customise other aspects of your report, click the relevant tab and complete the associated fields accordingly.

For instance, to specify which categories are excluded, click the Include tab. In the Select to include field, click those categories you *don't* want included.

Finally, carry out step 9.

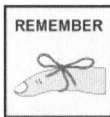

REMEMBER

By default, all accounts are selected for inclusion in the report. To exclude all accounts of a specific type, follow step 7. To further exclude *specific* accounts, carry out step 8.

Follow steps 1-4 (as appropriate) on page 158. Now do the following:

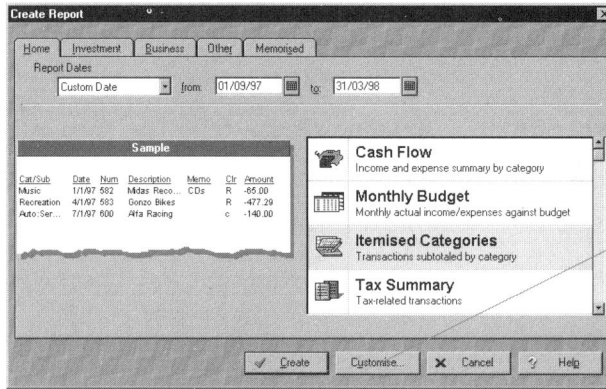

5 Click here

6 Ensure this tab is active

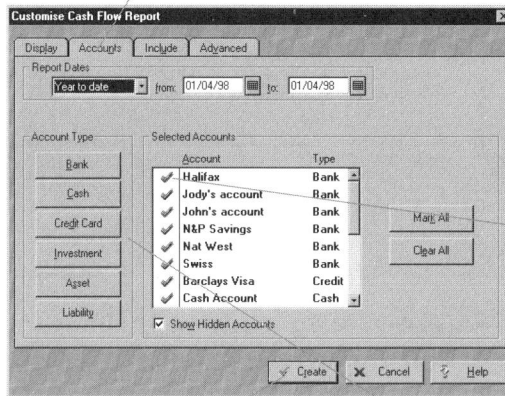

8 To exclude an account, click it

9 Click here to create the customised report

7 Click a button here to exclude an overall account type

Memorising reports

To recall a memorised report, pull down the Reports menu and click Memorised Reports. The Create Report dialog launches, with the Memorised tab active. Do the following:

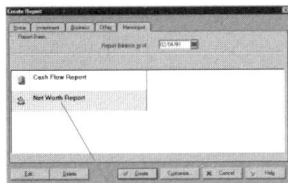

You can save reports you've already created for later use – Quicken calls this 'memorising'.

Memorising a report

Within the created report, do the following:

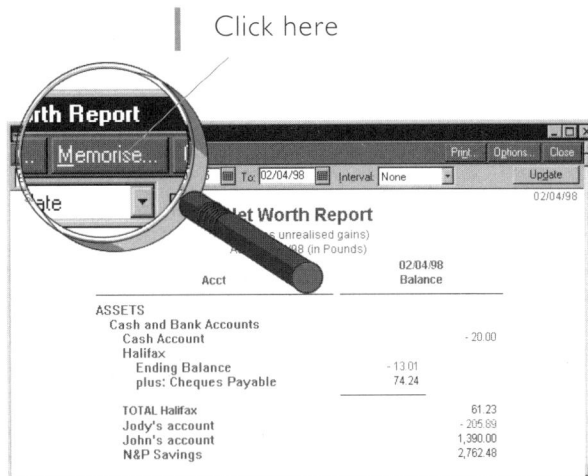

Click here

Double-click a report

rth Report

Memorise...

Print... Options... Close

To: 02/04/98   Interval: None   Update

02/04/98

Net Worth Report

(s unrealised gains)

98 (in Pounds)

	02/04/98
Acct	Balance

ASSETS
Cash and Bank Accounts
Cash Account — 20.00
Halifax
Ending Balance - 13.01
plus: Cheques Payable 74.24

TOTAL Halifax 61.23
Jody's account - 205.89
John's account 1,390.00
N&P Savings 2,762.48

HANDY TIP

Step 3 specifies the date range applied to memorised reports when reopened:

- Named Range is only available if the report was created with a preset date range (e.g. 'Year to date')
- Custom perpetuates any specific date range you've applied
- None uses the default date range imposed in step 5 on page 154

2 Name the saved report

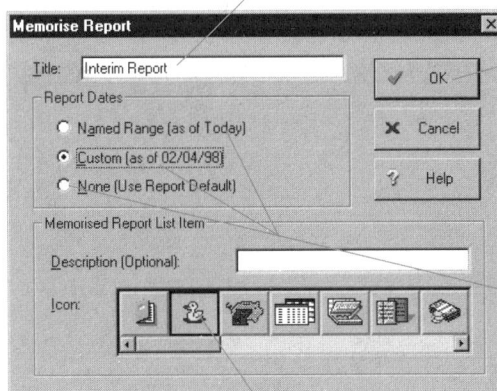

Memorise Report

Title: Interim Report

Report Dates
- Named Range (as of Today)
- Custom (as of 02/04/98)
- None (Use Report Default)

Memorised Report List Item
Description (Optional):

Icon:

✓ OK
✗ Cancel
? Help

5 Click here

3 Click a date range

4 Select an icon

Getting ready to print reports

It's often helpful to print out reports. However, before you can do this you need to:

* make sure the correct printer is selected

* specify page margins

* ensure your printer's settings are adjusted correctly

Report setup
Pull down the File menu and do the following:

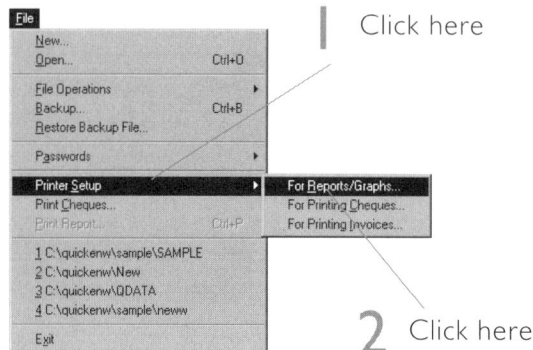

Click here

Click here

HANDY TIP

Click the Settings button to adjust your printer's internal settings (for how to do this, see your printer's manual).

Finally, follow step 5.

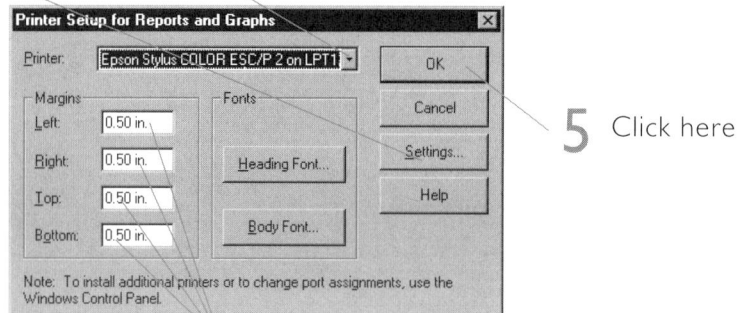

3 Click here; select a printer from the list

5 Click here

4 Adjust any of these to set revised margins

Report printing

Once you've generated a report, you can:

1. preview it (to make sure it's correct before you carry out 2 or 3 below) – see page 167

2. save it to disk as a separate file, in any of several formats

3. print it out

Step 2 above offers the following file formats:

ASCII   the most basic option. ASCII strips out all formatting; only the underlying data remains

Tab-delimited   a special format designed to be read by most word processors, spreadsheets and databases

1-2-3 PRN   mimics Lotus 1-2-3's proprietary format. Can also be read by programs which can import this format

Starting to print a report

After you've created a report – and after you've followed the procedures on page 164 – do the following to print it.

Click here

Carry out steps 1-3 below, as appropriate, then step 8. Alternatively, perform steps 4-7 to produce a disk-based report.

1 Click here for a paper-based report

HANDY TIP

If you want to preview your report before printing it, only follow steps 1-3 (as appropriate). Then carry out the procedures on page 167.

REMEMBER

Re step 3 – Draft Mode forces Quicken to print the report in a typeface resident within your printer – this is likely to be Courier. The result is quicker (though arguably less attractive) printing.

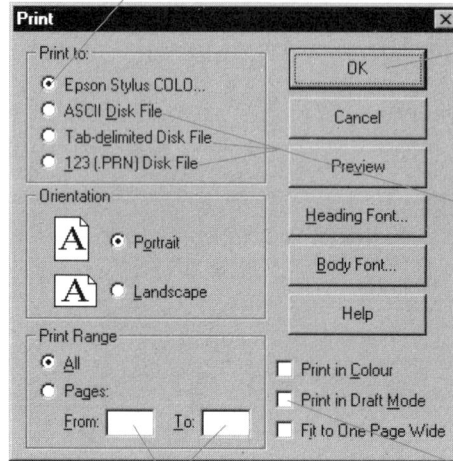

8 Click here to begin printing

4 Click any of these for a disk-based report (then carry out steps 5-7)

2 Type in start and end page numbers if you don't want to print the entire report

3 Click here to print in draft

7 Click here

6 Name the report file

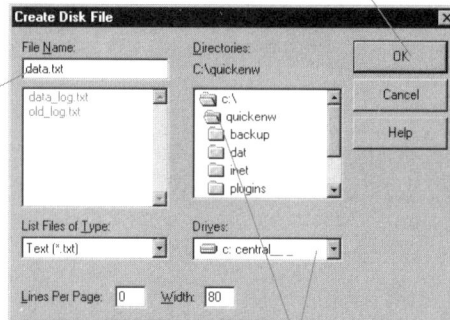

5 Click a drive/folder

Report previewing

You can preview a report before you print it, to verify that it meets your requirements.

Previewing a report

Follow the procedure on page 165 to launch the Print dialog. Carry out steps 1-3 on page 166, as appropriate. Now do the following:

HANDY TIP

To zoom in (magnify) or zoom out (shrink) the Preview window, move the mouse cursor:

Click here

to the relevant location and left-click once.

Repeat to reverse the action.

The Preview window launches. Do either of the following:

Click here (if available) to jump to the next page

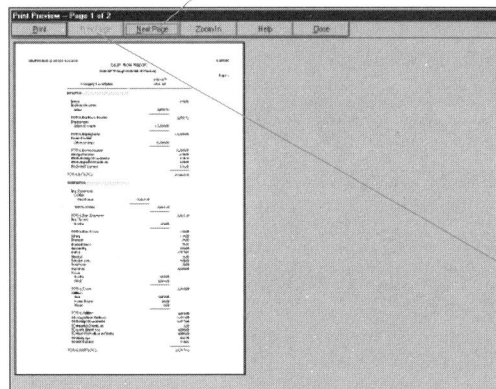

REMEMBER

When you're ready to print your report, click this button:

Print

Or press Esc to close the Preview window without printing, and return to your report.

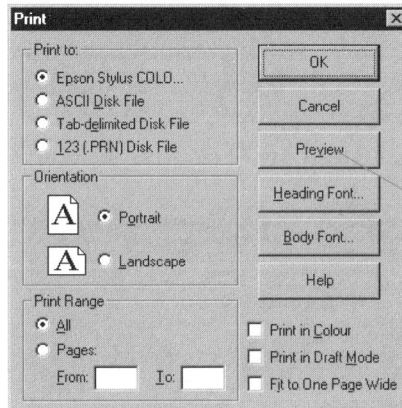

Click here (if available) to jump to the previous page

Graph types

Use graphs to achieve a visual overview of your finances.

Quicken's graphs are organised into four broad types, of which the following are applicable here:

- Income and Expense

- Net Worth

Income and Expense

Income and Expense graphs provide a visual model of your expenses, and compare them with your income over time. When these elements are displayed on screen, it's easier to compare them and reach valid conclusions.

REMEMBER

This is the graph Customise bar: a useful aid which lets you apply date ranges to graphs on-the-fly.

(See page 169 for how to hide the Customise bar.)

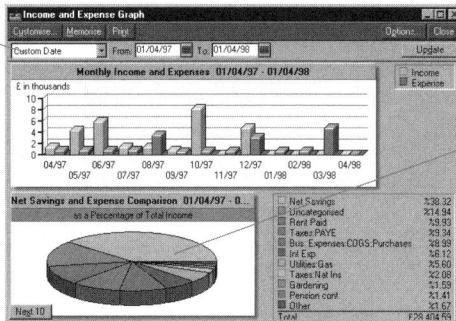

Pie chart – see the HANDY TIP

Net Worth

Net Worth graphs display your assets, liabilities and net worth for easy comparison. Use them to gain a vivid appreciation of your current outstanding debts.

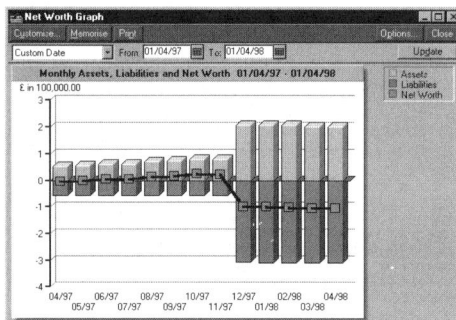

HANDY TIP

If you have more than 10 expenses, the pie chart component of the Income and Expense graph has this button in the bottom left-hand corner:

Next 10

Click it to have the pie chart reflect the next 10 expenses.

Graph settings

REMEMBER

Quicken graphs often consist of two components. However, you can – if you want – opt to display each part in its own window (for instance, so you can print them separately).

You can specify the following graph attributes:

- whether graphs display in separate windows

- whether graphs display and print two- or three-dimensionally (the two-dimensional option is useful if you're using a slow computer)

- whether graphs display in patterns or colours

Setting graph preferences

Pull down the Edit menu and do the following:

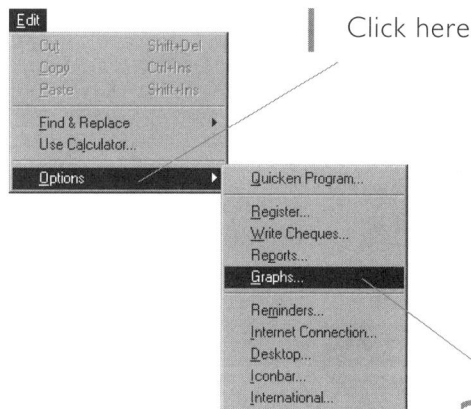

Click here

2 Click here

HANDY TIP

You can also opt to hide the Customise bar – simply click here:

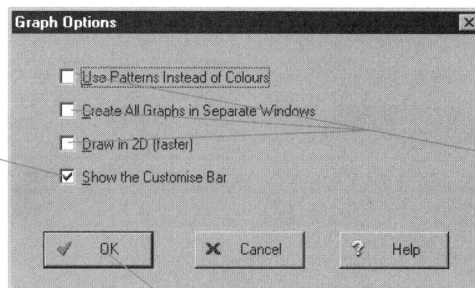

3 Select or deselect the appropriate options

4 Click here

Creating a graph

HANDY TIP

To memorise a graph you've created for later use, generate it in the normal way. Then click this button:

Memorise

in the overhead bar. In the Memorise Graph dialog, type in a name for the graph. Click OK.

HANDY TIP

To recall a memorised graph, pull down the Reports menu and click Graphs, Memorised Graphs. In the Memorised Graphs dialog, double-click a graph to reopen it. Use the Recall Memorised Graph dialog to specify the graph parameters (e.g. the date range and which accounts, categories and/or classes should be excluded)
Finally, click Create.

Generating a graph in Quicken is easy.

When you create a graph, you can:

- impose a start and end date (to exclude unnecessary transactions)

- specify which accounts, categories and/or classes should be included

- include or exclude associated sub-categories

- specify the graph type

Generating a graph

Pull down the Reports menu and do the following:

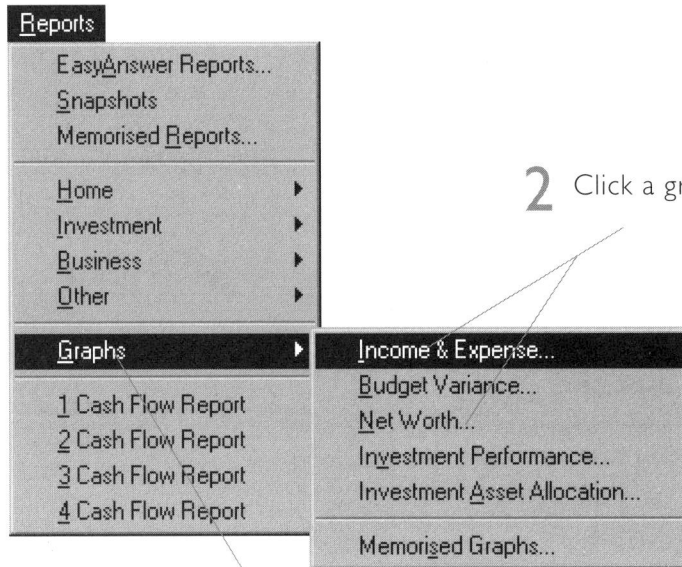

Reports

EasyAnswer Reports...
Snapshots
Memorised Reports...

Home   ▶
Investment   ▶
Business   ▶
Other   ▶

Graphs   ▶ | Income & Expense...
                   | Budget Variance...
1 Cash Flow Report | Net Worth...
2 Cash Flow Report | Investment Performance...
3 Cash Flow Report | Investment Asset Allocation...
4 Cash Flow Report |
                   | Memorised Graphs...

2 Click a graph type

Click here

Now carry out the additional steps on page 171.

...cont'd

Now follow steps 3-4 below.

Follow step 6 to exclude accounts from the graph. Then click one or more accounts to deselect them.

Finally, carry out step 9 to create the graph.

Follow step 7 to exclude categories or sub-categories from the graph. Then click one or more categories/ sub-categories to deselect them.

Finally, carry out step 9 to create the graph.

Follow step 8 to exclude classes or sub-classes from the graph. Then click one or more classes/sub-classes to deselect them.

Finally, carry out step 9 to create the graph.

3 Type in start and end dates

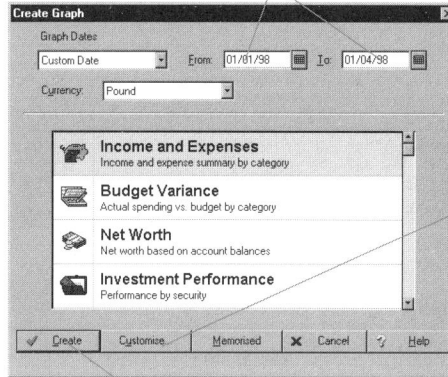

5 Click here

4 Click here

Customising graphs

If you need to produce a customised graph, follow step 5 above (but not 3-4). Now do the following, as appropriate (refer to the REMEMBER tips for assistance):

6 Click here   7 Click here   8 Click here

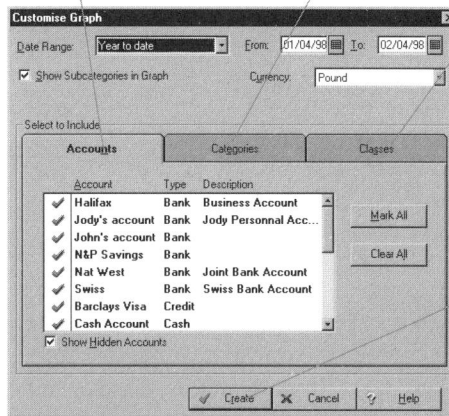

9 Click here

Creating an EasyAnswer graph

To view an EasyAnswer graph, pull down the Reports menu and carry out the following steps:

Reports

EasyAnswer Reports...
Snapshots
Memorised Reports...
Home ▶
Investment ▶
Business ▶
Other ▶
Graphs ▶
1 Cash Flow Report
2 Itemised Categories Report
3 Itemised Categories Report
4 Cash Flow Report

REMEMBER

See pages 159-160 for how to create EasyAnswer reports.

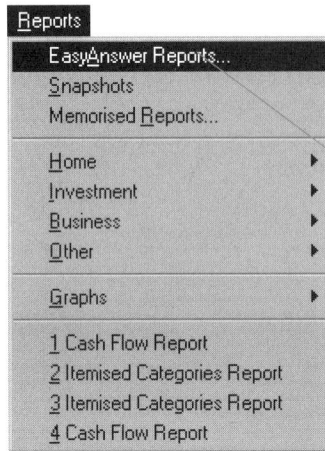

Click here

2 Click a question

3 Complete any subsidiary fields

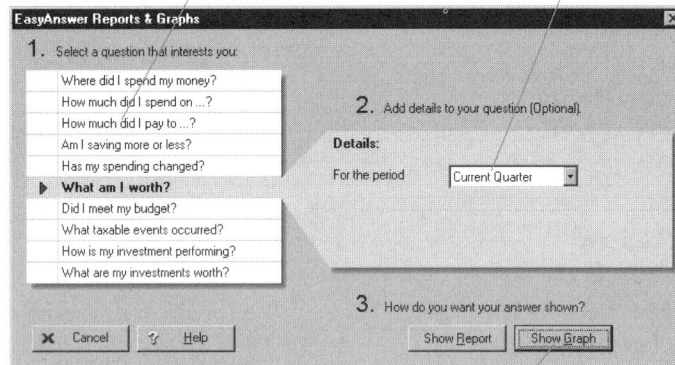

EasyAnswer Reports & Graphs

1. Select a question that interests you:

- Where did I spend my money?
- How much did I spend on ...?
- How much did I pay to ...?
- Am I saving more or less?
- Has my spending changed?
- **What am I worth?**
- Did I meet my budget?
- What taxable events occurred?
- How is my investment performing?
- What are my investments worth?

2. Add details to your question (Optional).

Details:

For the period   Current Quarter

3. How do you want your answer shown?

✕ Cancel   ? Help   Show Report   Show Graph

4 Click here

Working with graphs

When you've created a graph, you can use a Quicken feature called QuickZoom to:

- produce a graphical breakdown of a selected graph component

- produce a transaction report relating to the specified component

Quicken decides which of these options is most appropriate in any given circumstance.

You can also use QuickZoom to:

- hide a specific graph component

- make a graph component display its associated numerical value

REMEMBER

Hiding graph components doesn't erase them: it simply makes them invisible.

Producing a breakdown/report

After you've created a graph, move the mouse pointer over a graph component (the pointer changes to a magnifying glass). Then carry out the following:

Double-click here

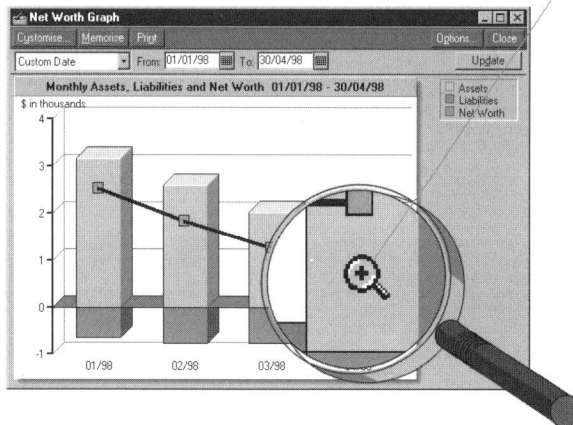

HANDY TIP

If this technique produces a report, press Esc twice to return to the original graph.

To undo a hide operation, click this button:

Update

This makes all graph components visible again.

Hiding a graph component

After you've created a graph, move the mouse pointer over a graph component (the pointer changes to a magnifying glass). Then carry out the following to hide it:

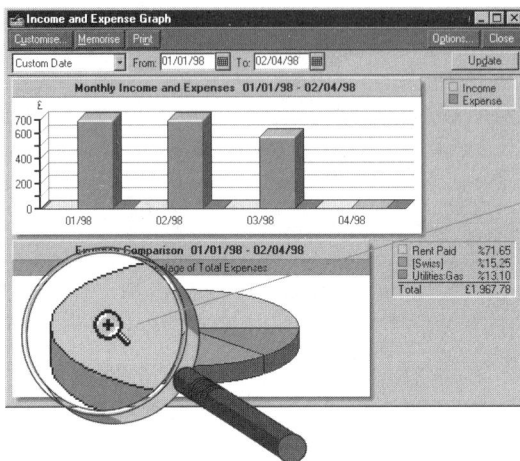

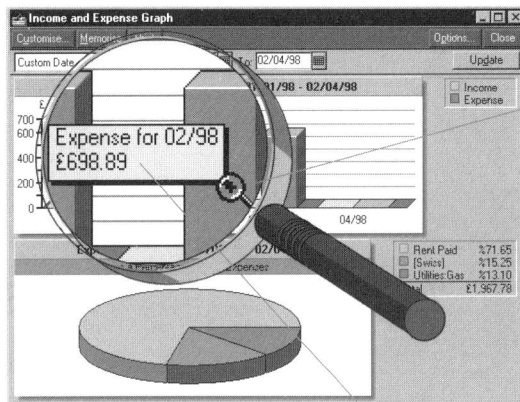

Hold down Shift and left-click here

Producing numerical equivalents

After you've created a graph, move the mouse pointer over a graph component (the pointer changes to a magnifying glass). Then carry out the following:

Keep the mouse pointer stationary and wait a few seconds

The numerical equivalent (and explanatory text)

Getting ready to print graphs

You may well want to print out your graphs. However, before you can do this you need to:

- make sure the correct printer is selected

- specify page margins

- ensure your printer's settings are adjusted correctly

Graph setup
Pull down the File menu and do the following:

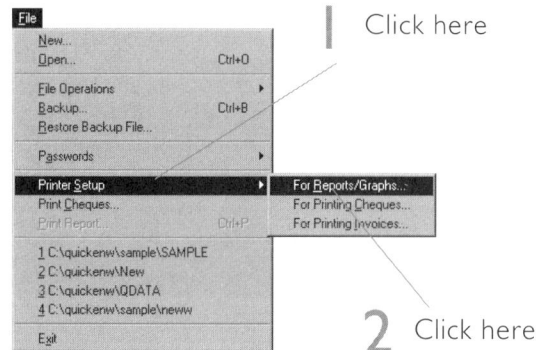

Click here

1

2 Click here

HANDY TIP

Click the Settings button to adjust your printer's internal settings (for how to do this, see your printer's manual). Finally, follow step 5.

3 Click here; select a printer from the list

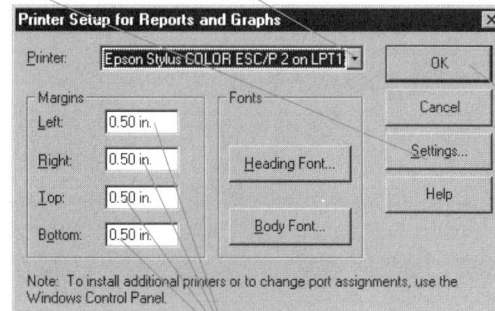

5 Click here

4 Adjust any of these to set revised margins

Printing graphs

Once you've customised graph printer setup, it's easy to print out your graph.

However, you should note that when you tell Quicken to print a graph, printing begins immediately (there is no intervening dialog) providing that:

- your printer has been switched on and is on-line

- enough paper has been inserted

Printing is also subject to the graph settings described on page 169.

Starting to print

Make sure your printer is ready to begin printing (see the provisos above), and that the graph you want to print is active.

Now pull down the File menu and perform step 1 below:

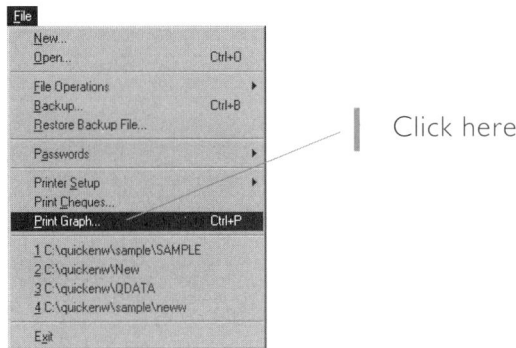

```
File
   New...
   Open...                        Ctrl+O

   File Operations            ▶
   Backup...                      Ctrl+B
   Restore Backup File...

   Passwords                  ▶

   Printer Setup              ▶
   Print Cheques...
   Print Graph...                 Ctrl+P

   1 C:\quickenw\sample\SAMPLE
   2 C:\quickenw\New
   3 C:\quickenw\QDATA
   4 C:\quickenw\sample\neww

   Exit
```

Click here

Alternatively, refer to the bar at the head of the graph and carry out step 2 below:

```
Customise...  Memorise  Print                          Options...  Close
```

2 Click here

Advanced Use

Use this chapter to learn how to set and track budgets, and to use budget reports and graphs. Then you'll use the Financial Calendar to gain a visual overview of your present and future finances; add notes to the Financial Calendar; preview it; and then print it out. Finally, you'll connect to the World Wide Web directly from within Quicken.

Covers

Chapter Nine

Budgets – an overview

You can use Quicken to set up – and use – budgets. In Quicken, budgeting revolves around categories.

After using Quicken over a period of time, you'll probably have created categories which are tailor-made to fit in with your own finances; you can use these (and other categories) for budget tracking. However, before you create your first budget, it's a good idea to review your category list. In particular:

You can also insert budget amounts yourself, if you want.

1. ensure that categories exist for income or expenses you want to budget

2. consider deleting categories you haven't used, and aren't likely to

At its simplest, creating a budget involves:

— (if necessary) clearing any previous data in the budget

When Quicken auto-creates a budget based on past account entries (see step 4 on page 179), you can choose from two options:

- Use Monthly Detail makes Quicken transfer actual values into their corresponding budget months

- Use Average for Period ensures that Quicken inserts average values

— having Quicken insert budget amounts based on actual income and outgoings you've recorded in Quicken (this process is called autocreation)

Once you've created a budget, you can:

— monitor budget progress on-the-fly, with the Progress bar

— generate a budget report (this relates your budget amounts to the amounts you received or spent, and calculates the difference)

— have Quicken create a budget variance graph. This compares income/spending with budgeted spending and helps you answer these questions:

A. is your budget working?

B. how accurate have your budget estimate been?

C. where are you overspending or underspending?

Creating a budget

Pull down the Features menu and click Planning, Budgets. Now do the following:

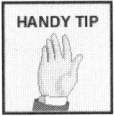 **If you need to clear previous budget amounts, follow step 1. In the menu, click Clear All.** Then carry out steps 1-2.

 **To save your budget when you've finished creating it, click this button:**

Save

 **Re step 3 – enter dates in this format:**

month/year

 **Only carry out step 5 if you *don't* want the budget to apply to all categories.** If you do follow step 5, also perform steps 7-8 on page 180.

1 Click here

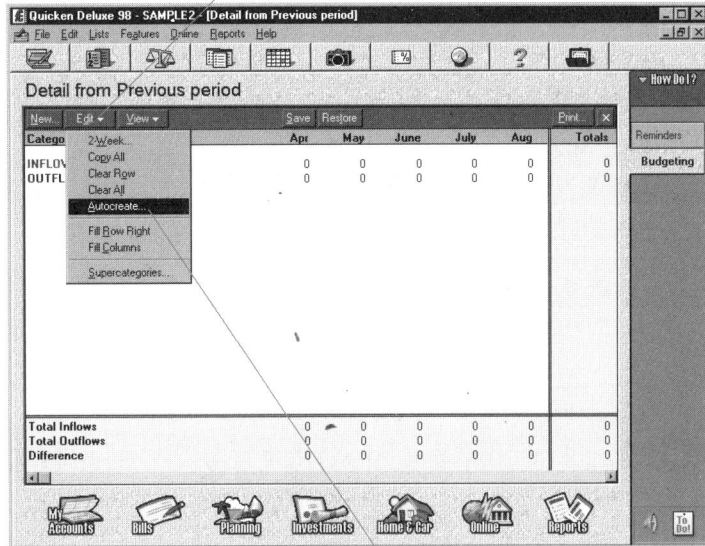

2 Click here

3 Enter start and end dates

6 Click here

5 Click here

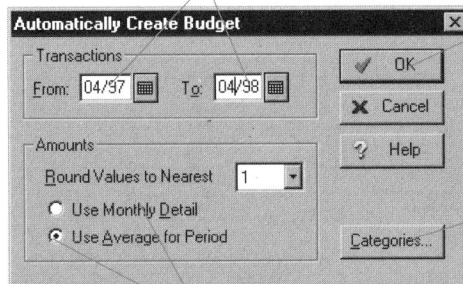

4 Click one of these (see the REMEMBER tip on page 178)

Now carry out the following additional steps:

7 To exclude a category
from the budget, click it

REMEMBER

Repeat step 7 as often as necessary, then carry out step 8.

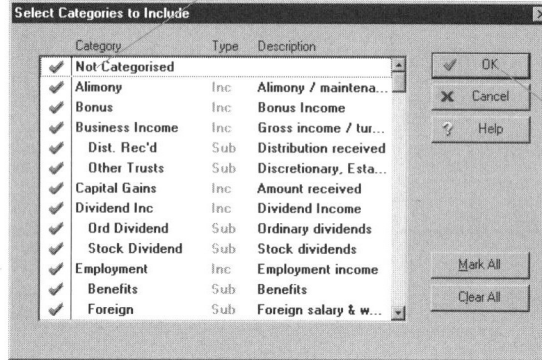

Select Categories to Include				
Category	Type	Description		
✓ Not Categorised			✓ OK	
✓ Alimony	Inc	Alimony / maintena...	✗ Cancel	
✓ Bonus	Inc	Bonus Income		
✓ Business Income	Inc	Gross income / tur...	? Help	
✓ Dist. Rec'd	Sub	Distribution received		
✓ Other Trusts	Sub	Discretionary, Esta...		
✓ Capital Gains	Inc	Amount received		
✓ Dividend Inc	Inc	Dividend Income		
✓ Ord Dividend	Sub	Ordinary dividends		
✓ Stock Dividend	Sub	Stock dividends		
✓ Employment	Inc	Employment income	Mark All	
✓ Benefits	Sub	Benefits		
✓ Foreign	Sub	Foreign salary & w...	Clear All	

8 Click here

The illustration below shows the auto-created budget:

HANDY TIP

If you want to amend any of these values manually, click in the appropriate field: then type in a revised value.

Quicken Deluxe 98 - SAMPLE2 - [Detail from Previous period]						
File Edit Lists Features Online Reports Help						
Detail from Previous period						▼ How Do I?
New...	Edit ▼	View ▼		Save	Restore	Print... ×
Category View	Apr	May	June	July	Aug	Totals
INFLOWS						
Bonus	18	18	18	18	18	216
Business income	229	229	229	229	229	2748
Employment	948	948	948	948	948	11376
Invest. income	635	635	635	635	635	7620
Old Age Pension	-17	-17	-17	-17	-17	-204
OthCapGnDst	364	364	364	364	364	4368
OUTFLOWS						
Bus. Expenses	-196	-196	-196	-196	-196	-2352
Bus. Taxes	-10	-10	-10	-10	-10	-120
Dining	-9	-9	-9	-9	-9	-108
Entertain	-4	-4	-4	-4	-4	-48
Entertainment	-6	-6	-6	-6	-6	-72
Gardening	-35	-35	-35	-35	-35	-420
Int Exp	-134	-134	-134	-134	-134	-1608
Medical	-1	-1	-1	-1	-1	-12
Pension cont.	-31	-31	-31	-31	-31	-372
Total Inflows	2177	2177	2177	2177	2177	26124
Total Outflows	-1022	-1022	-1022	-1022	-1022	-12264
Difference	1155	1155	1155	1155	1155	13860

Tracking your budget

You can monitor budget progress in three ways:

- through the use of the Progress Bar, an on-screen gauge

- by creating budget reports

- by creating budget variance graphs

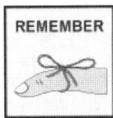

REMEMBER

The Progress bar displays irrespective of whether QuickTabs are on-screen (but the colour changes).

Using the Progress bar

To make the Progress bar visible, pull down the Features menu and click Planning, Progress Bars. The Progress bar displays at the base of the screen:

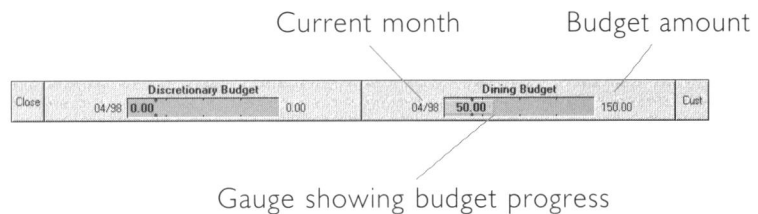

Current month   Budget amount

Close	Discretionary Budget		Dining Budget		Cust
	04/98	0.00	0.00	04/98	50.00	150.00	

Gauge showing budget progress

Here, the Progress bar is tracking a budget set up to monitor outgoings in respect of the Dining category. The current month is shown on the left, and the relevant budget amount on the right. The active gauge is shown in more detail below:

HANDY TIP

You can vary the budget period. Click this button:

View ▼

In the menu which launches, click one of these:

- Months
- Quarters
- Year

These arrows show where your budget should be

50.00

This is the actual spending figure for the budget period (in this case, the current month)

HANDY TIP

You can produce a report in more depth by following a different procedure.

Pull down the Reports menu and click Other, Budget. Now complete the Create Report dialog in line with steps 4-8 on page 158. (Alternatively, perform steps 5-9 on page 162 to customise the report).

HANDY TIP

You can also produce a budget graph using the EasyAnswer dialog above.

Simply click this button:

Show Graph

The result is a budget variance graph:

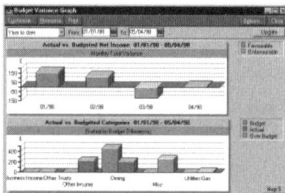

Generating budget reports

To view a statement of how your budget is progressing, pull down the Reports menu and click EasyAnswer. Now do the following:

1 Click here   2 Select a period

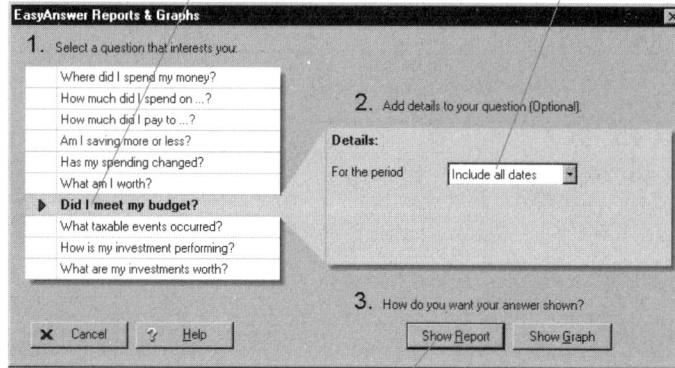

3 Click here

Generating budget variance graphs

Budget variance graphs help you answer these questions:

— Is your budget working (viewed from month to month)?

— Are your spending estimates accurate?

— If you're overspending or underspending, in what categories?

Pull down the Reports menu and click Graphs, Budget Variance. Now do ONE of the following:

- to create a standard graph, follow steps 3-4 on page 171

- to create a customised graph, follow steps 5-9 on page 171

Using the Financial Calendar

You can use the Financial Calendar – a way of viewing your finances visually – to enter and view regular deposits and expenses. The Financial Calendar displays forthcoming transactions, too.

Displaying the Financial Calendar

Pull down the Features menu and do the following:

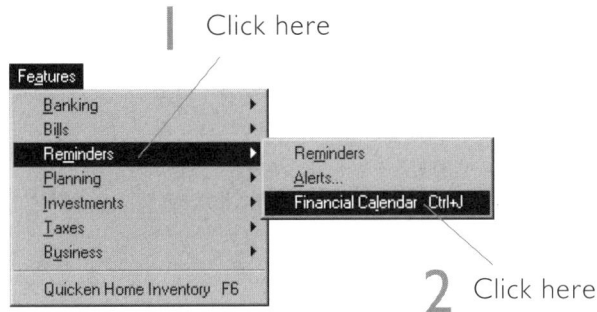

Click here

| Features |
| Banking ▶ |
| Bills ▶ |
Reminders ▶	Reminders
Planning ▶	Alerts...
Investments ▶	Financial Calendar Ctrl+J
Taxes ▶
Business ▶
Quicken Home Inventory F6

2 Click here

REMEMBER

For how to enter standing orders/ direct debits, see page 104.

Entering a non-recurring transaction

To enter one-off transactions via the Financial Calendar, do the following:

HANDY TIP

Use these buttons: to jump to a different month.

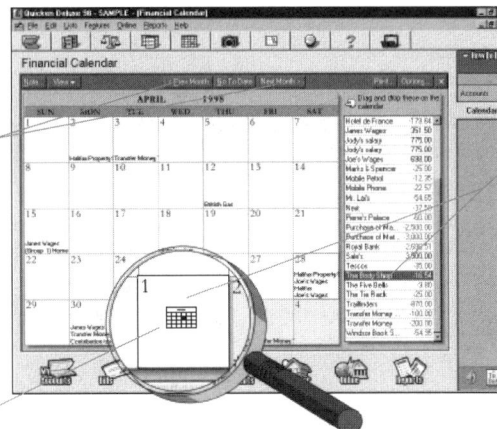

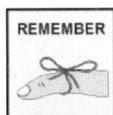

REMEMBER

The Calendar icon: signifies that you're about to insert a transaction.

Click a transaction in the list; drag it to the relevant date

Now carry out the additional steps on page 184.

...cont'd

HANDY TIP

Ensure Register Transaction is active.

HANDY TIP

Dates with associated notes look like this:

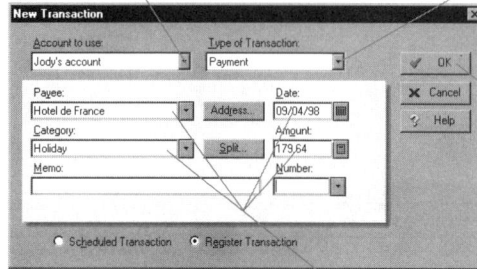

9

This represents a note

To display the note (for reading or editing), click the note symbol (see above).

HANDY TIP

For how to complete the Print dialog, see page 166 (but note that not all the options are available here).

HANDY TIP

To preview your Calendar before printing, click the Preview button in the Print dialog. To print the Calendar, click Print.

Now carry out the additional steps below:

2 Click here; select an account in the list

3 Click here; select a payment type in the list

New Transaction

Account to use: Jody's account

Type of Transaction: Payment

✓ OK

Payee: Hotel de France — Address...

Date: 09/04/98

✗ Cancel

Category: Holiday — Split...

Amount: 179,64

? Help

Memo:

Number:

○ Scheduled Transaction   ● Register Transaction

5 Click here

4 Complete these fields

Adding notes to the Financial Calendar

You can associate notes with specific dates. To do this, right-click the date. In the menu, click Note. Do the following:

1 Type in the note

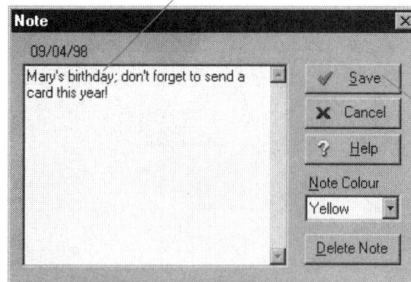

Note

09/04/98

Mary's birthday; don't forget to send a card this year!

✓ Save

✗ Cancel

? Help

Note Colour: Yellow

Delete Note

2 Click here

Printing the Financial Calendar

Press Ctrl+P. Then complete the Print dialog, as appropriate. Click OK to begin printing.

Using Snapshots

Quicken has another feature you can use to take a visual overview of your finances: Snapshots. Snapshots display multiple aspects of your finances, graphically and in a single screen.

For instance, you can view:

*   Net Worth graphs

*   Income and Expense graphs

*   Expense Comparison graphs

*   Budget progress gauges

*   Financial Calendar Notes

simultaneously.

You can:

—   specify which snapshots display where

—   specify whether each snapshot is graphic- or text-based

—   enlarge any snapshot, if desired (except notes)

Launching the Snapshots screen

Refer to the overhead Iconbar and do the following:

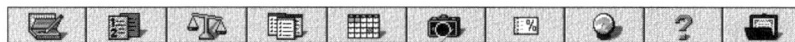

Click here

Alternatively, pull down the Reports menu and click Snapshots.

...cont'd

HANDY TIP

To print out your snapshots, press Ctrl+P. Printing begins immediately.

HANDY TIP

To further customise the snapshot selected in step 1 (i.e. to specify which accounts, categories and/or classes are excluded), click this button after you've carried out step 4:

Customise Snapshot...

Now complete the dialog which launches. Click OK. Finally, follow step 5.

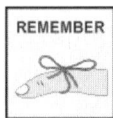

REMEMBER

After step A, the snapshot expands:

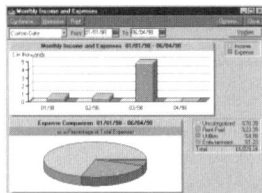

Press Esc to close it.

Specifying a snapshot
Carry out the following steps:

2 Click here

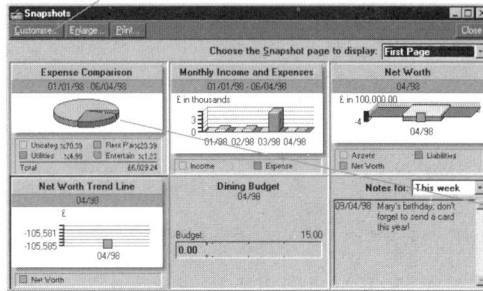

Click a snapshot

3 Click a snapshot type

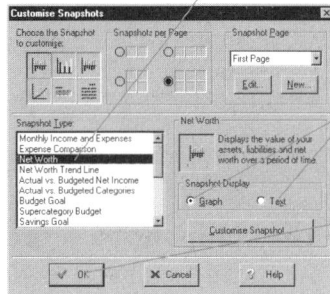

4 Click one of these

5 Click here

Enlarging a snapshot
Position the mouse pointer over a snapshot and do the following:

A Double-click here

Connecting to the World Wide Web

You can use Quicken to access Intuit's Web site directly. When you've done so, you have access to an assortment of associated services. These include:

- general financial news
- mortgage advice
- information on savings and borrowings
- pensions information
- details of currency markets
- information on specific Intuit products (Quicken and QuickBooks), and technical support

Accessing the Web

First, connect to your service provider in the usual way. Then do the following:

REMEMBER

To access the Internet from within Quicken, you must have:

- an Internet connection (ie you must have installed a modem or, an ISDN line, etc.)
- registered with an Internet Service Provider (e.g. MSN)

(For information on the Internet in general, consult a companion volume: 'Internet UK in easy steps'.)

BEWARE

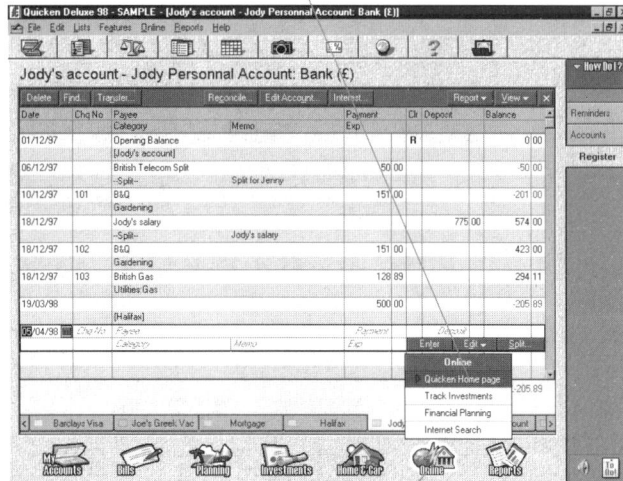

The first time you use Quicken to connect to the Web, you may have to complete a series of setup dialogs first. Simply follow the on-screen instructions.

2 Click here

Place the mouse pointer here

...cont'd

This is the result. Carry out the following steps:

3 Click a service

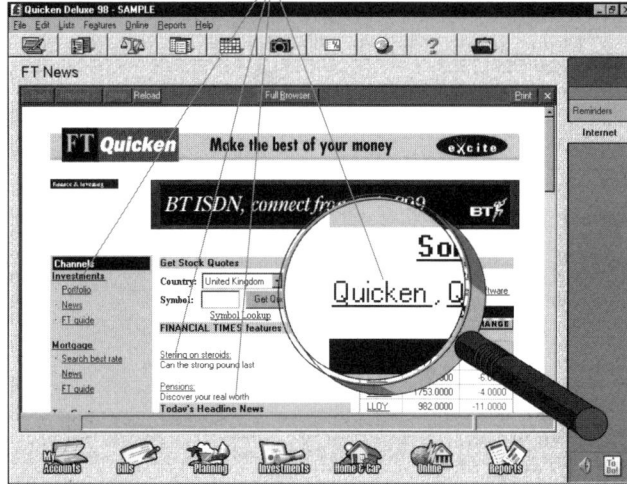

HANDY TIP

Quicken displays Web screens *directly* **(your browser is loaded behind the scenes).**

This is the result of clicking on Quicken (see above):

REMEMBER

To close down your Quicken Internet session, click this button:

X

in the top right-hand corner of the Quicken screen.

(Don't forget to close the connection to your provider, too.)

The Quicken UK Web site

Index